The Poet's Domain

The Poet's Domain

Collection of Poems

Volume Twenty

A Slice of Life

Compiled and edited by
Patricia S. Adler

Live Wire Press
1-866-579-3850
http://www.livewirepress.net

Compiled and edited by
Patricia S. Adler

Cover art: Acrylic painting on Italian tile © by Terry Cox-Joseph

For information write:
Live Wire Press
2657 Jefferson Park Circle
Charlottesville, Virginia 22903
e-mail: padler@cstone.net
Web site: http://www.livewirepress.net

If you are unable to order this book from your local bookseller, you may order directly from the publisher. Call 1-866-579-3850 toll free.

Library of Congress Cataloging-in-Publication Data

A Slice of Life . . ./ compiled and edited by Patricia S. Adler.
p. cm. — (The poet's domain ; v. 20)
ISBN 0-9672885-9-2 (alk. paper)
1. American poetry—Middle Atlantic States. 2. American poetry—20th century. 3. Millay, Edna St. Vincent, 1895-1950. First fig—Poetry. I. Adler, Patricia S., 1938- . II. Series.
PS545.M9 2001
811'.6080974—dc21

2001005477

10 9 8 7 6 5 4 3 2 1

Printed on recycled acid-free paper in the United States

Dedication

To the ancients, muses, guides, guardians—
present and future seers of Truth.

Table of Contents

Editor's Note

The many entries that appear in this volume are so varied in theme, it gave me pause to sift out a general theme in order to give the volume a name or title.

I realized after reviewing the entries that they mirror your hearts. This volume is a kaleidoscope of hope and despair, gratitude and regret, nostalgia and longing, loneliness and fear; in short, your ecstasies and agonies.

I sincerely thank you for sharing such personal work. You will find entries that are jewels of expression and form. You will also find entries that lack polish and lustre. I beg your indulgence in forming this mélange, and ask you to withhold judgement of form to consider the sentiment expressed.

Once again it is my pleasure and honor to bring this work forward.

Patricia S. Adler
Publisher

Condom Conundrum

Under the spreading tree of life
the pontiff contemplates
a dire dilemma:
protection for life that may never be
vs
possible death for life extant.
Procreative use enjoined.
The clergy smile.
Recreation
escapes
purview.

Barbara H. Achilles

(b.1931, Knowlesville, N.Y.), former music director and script writer and a retired Intelligence Officer, graduated from the Eastman School of Music and the College of Arts and Sciences, University of Rochester. Her poetry has appeared in volumes 5–20 of *The Poet's Domain*, and in The *Wall Street Journal*. She has been Moderator of the Poets of Tallwood workshop of the Learning in Retirement Institute at George Mason University since 1997 and is a member of the National League of American Pen Women. She is a resident of Vienna, Va.

The Organist's Lament

Johann Sebastian Bach
was a musical genius—it's true.
Weaving his intricate tapestries
from a rich contrapuntal menu.
But from years of review
and construing his craft,
we have not yet truly discerned
why he put the most technically difficult notes
at the point where a page must be turned.

Barbara H. Achilles

Time Out

I love a snowless winter. Sun subdued
and colors grayed. Air cleansed of dank, impure
miasmic waste. Long days to mend and cure—
when time is slow and chores no more are queued.
When trees have dropped their leaves and
limbs protrude
that once were clothed in vivid *haute couture*
and grass is frozen in a stark gravure
that nature etched in mystic quietude.
A time to sit and contemplate the world.
To sift the memories of tears and love
of all things good and bad that filled the hours,
so when old joys and sorrows have been furled
and we again can see bright stars above,
we know new life is well within our powers.

Sisyphus at the Supermarket

Alone
on the loading platform
he bravely copes with
the frenzied assault
of the afternoon trade
scrambling for their groceries.
At the same time
he polices the area,
pushing telescoped trains of empties
up the ramp to the cart park,
where a new contingent of shoppers
awaits
to start the cycle again.

Barbara H. Achilles

Neighborhood Watch

Sed quis custodiet ipsos Custodes*

The patrol comes on little cat paws
A golden tiger burning bright,
checking out the premises,
sniffing bush and tree
for signs of interlopers.

He positions himself
in an unplanted planter
at the top of the red brick steps,
assumes the pose of the Great Sphinx
and turns his attention towards
a cluster of suspicious sparrows
twittering in a nearby tree.

He keeps them under close surveillance
looking for a lapse in alertness
that might signal lunch.
No luck
He rolls on his back
for an afternoon snooze.
The only crime today
will be cat-napping.

*But who will watch the watchers?
—Juvenal. *Satires VI*

Trust

I dance around the dark edges
of your abyss,
drawn to the darkness—
curious, fascinated.
If I should fly
into the darkness
how far would I fall?
As far as I want?
Or will you draw me
to the bottom,
into your wound?
And then?
Would I ever
be free again
to dance
where I will?

Patricia. S. Adler

(b. 1938, Elizabeth, N.J.) is editing, typesetting, weaving in the world of words and language, painting, singing, and investigating the healing arts. Her poetry has been published in many volumes of *The Poet's Domain.*

Of Time and Silas*

Old man, the woods wherein you walk tonight,
Are they as dark, as lovely deep as those
You yearned? What moons rise over virgin paths?
How silent is the wind, how tall the trees?
We seek some deeper thought behind the words
You wrote, encompass words with thoughts you may
Have little dreamed, or dreaming, little cared.
We cannot track you through the drifted span,
And stones to lift and walls to mend are chores,
Or legacies, for men to cope with here.

That night, did you have far to go to home?
What Warren laid his hand on your last breath
Iambic-metering out? Did white sails move
Hull down on moonlit skies? The miles all spent,
The promise kept, did you—home safely now,
With Mary's ilk close by—slip past the door
Or through the half-raised window down to where
The pale trees beckoned at the winter's edge
To swingers of birches? There are things worse.
We shall not grieve. You move in soundless woods
And weeping is of time and Silas' form.

Kate W. Anderson

Born in North Carolina, she has lived all but four years of her life in Virginia. As a junior in high school, she was awarded the Class A State Championship in poetry. Her poems have received awards, including two first places in the Irene Leach Memorial Contest. She at one time was a staff reporter on the *Norfolk Ledger Star*, as well as the *Portsmouth Ledger Star* and a member of the Virginia Press Association. She is a member of the Poetry Society of Virginia and has also won awards for her paintings. She is currently at work on a novel.

*as Robert Frost's death was announced

Flying with Icarus

In memory of Sylvia Plath

Join me singing
For our winged friends
Who have flown like
Icarus up the double
Helix lines until some
Errant gene tripped their
gentle madness,
Causing them to put
naming aside,
Causing prayers to end
In the teaming tyranny
of their minds.

Join me singing
For our soaring Sylvia,
Flying on her fragile
waxen wings,
Ever pushing sky edges
Where the light is brightest,
Where the exhilaration hides.
See her tucking two
sleeping babies
Into their warm beds,
Saying goodbye to "Daddy,"
Saying goodbye to "Ted,"
Lying comfortably on the
kitchen floor
After, turning on the
hissing gas.

Jason Lester Atkins

was born in Hampton, Va., and attended Huntington School of Engineering and the University of Oklahoma. He was a gunner on a torpedo bomber in WW II. His first published story appeared in *Holiday Magazine* in 1950. His published poetry has appeared in *The Poet's Domain*, *Borders*, *Writer's Voice*, *Beacon*, and *West Virginia Review*. He is now retired and is facilitator of the Virginia Beach Writer's Group.

Miscarriage

Your blood betrayed
my desire
to give you life,
to love your father
was not enough.

Did I work too hard,
exercise too much,
sleep or eat too little,
take too many vitamins—
or not enough?
Enough. Enough.

I look into your father's eyes—
my husband's—
to see beyond concern for me
into the vacancy of sorrow:
oceans of unshed tears
that I can never cross.

I wonder if he blames me.
"I'm sorry," I say—
silly, stupid . . .
pointless.
But there is no other way
to hide

this unsettling, natural terror
from this man,
while wanting him to understand.

As pieces of eternity
pass through me,
severed from what might have been,
I nurture this pain
that marks your life.

Dawn Bailiff

has "performed" her poetry in numerous solo shows, poetry series, and workshops, both for live and television audiences. Most recently, Dawn's work has appeared in *The Vietnam War Generation Journal*, *MS Connection*, and volume 19 of *The Poet's Domain*. Other publication credits include: *The Denver Quarterly*, *The Mind's Eye*, *Gothic*, *Atticus Review*, *Protea Poetry Journal*, and *The Ohio Review*. A graduate of the Peabody Conservatory in her native Baltimore, Dawn currently resides in Wilmington, Del. where she teaches classical piano, while completing her first novel.

Dawn Bailiff

Faith

It was easy to believe in God
when I could run and dance or even do a full
        day's work.
Now, it takes some effort to retrieve
        my soul
from the bottom of broken efforts MS makes
        of my life.

I am never certain who the real enemy is:
the voices who tell me I am not the same or
the disease that has made me believe it's so.

Sensation is a gift I no longer squander:
swallowing the steak without thinking.
Your kiss upon my skin. The smell of coffee.
How did a crying baby; a rainy Monday
        morning's thunder
become so charming?

When my fickle vision does not bob in cloudy
        water,
the flowers and the birds leap like magical
        gnomes,
from the pop-up pages of a masterful illustrator.

The longing is for my own strength—
like a virtuous woman I must woo it with
        gentleness.
If I struggle and demand, I will alienate her
        forever.

The God within me now cries out
to reach the God within others,
shrinking the importance of my cane, my
        crutches, or my chair.
I will avoid the temptation to get drunk
on hatred for those who cannot see past these props
        to the underlying plot.

Pity, however, is permissible,
for their blindness is much darker
than anything MS can dish out.

We hold onto familiar paradigms because they
are familiar,
not because they are good.

Monster

My eyes search your face for acceptance
Underneath your feigned compassion
Leaking fear.
Tingling; tremors;
Innervated limbs;
Paralyzing pain;
Legs frozen.
Eyes wide blind.
Short-term disability.
Cognitive loss
Loss, loss . . .
Energy oozing vacuous—never to
Return. Robbers ripping
Open wounds of misunderstanding. Alienation.
Slurred speech swimming past the
Insular Tahiti of the
Soul.

Dawn Bailiff

Penelope

Waiting for your return,
I sprinkle chaste tree leaves upon our marriage
bed
where now I only eat too much but lose weight
anyway—
longing gnaws so like a tapeworm.

I avoid the wine in fear
its fiery lips would coax me into doing
those things I dream
upon my lonely couch
of once simmering fires frozen
until they cut like ice—

although I did not know touch
before you. I never knew I could desire.

The aching in the soul of me is not a need for
Man . . .
but for you.
And you alone.
Each night my virtue is unwoven,
preserving me like the shroud
I pretend to weave
for your dead father:
vain labor forged
to seal out all those voices
that would make you dead.

Fragrant, pale and lilac-blue
my flower does not wither in the waiting
but pulls from the sweat of broken land
a quiet strength.

For Helen

Excavated palace walls buried
in miasma of rubbish heaps—
brittle parchment,
etched in camel dung,
cuneiform wedges to confuse
grave robbers,
pot shards, bone shank,
bricks cracked
into a thousand puzzles.

Bring seed cakes pungent
with the perfume of orange
and lemon rinds,
bitterroot hidden under
flowering pomegranates,
our last meal aromatic with cinnamon
coriander and honeyed
wine from the old king's
secret storehouse.

Did you expect me to give you plunder,
a pair of soft gold bracelets
to warm in your hands?
an amulet for your throat?

I'll leave, perhaps
the Trojan horse.

Doris C. Baker

Principal of an American Army school in Germany after World War II; master's degree from the University of Michigan; author of a novel, *The Originals*, 2002; poetry, short fiction, articles, and essays in The Poetry Society of Virginia *Anthology 2003*, *The Virginia Gazette*, *The Daily Press*, *Virginia Adversaria*, *Pegasus Review*, *Skylark*, *Sensations Magazine*, *German Life Magazine* and other publications; member of two Virginia Beach writers groups.

Landlocked

A thousand miles
from the scent of salt
and the rough caress

of the ocean's grip,
where the moon's just light
not the driver of tides

and the waves are just grain
that give in to the wind,
the lakes and the rivers

speak only in whispers
that cannot compel
stone to disrobe.

lorraine m. Benedetto

Child of the 60s born and raised in the North East, moved to Tidewater Virginia in '92, transferred to Wilmington, North Carolina in the fall of 2001, where I have begun to notice the influence of water and tides becoming more and more entrenched in my writing. Writer of poetry and short stories—with an ongoing attempt to complete my first full length novel. Previously published in *The Poet's Domain*, volumes 17 and 19; *Beacon;* and *Poetic Voices*.

lorraine m. Benedetto

Mis-Step

Steps that once progressed
in sheltered confidence
        faltered as the scenery
shifted to forgotten views.
Mortified, she realized
        her course had gone askew.

No bread crumbs of redemption
offered silent guidance; no eastern star
blazed on high
        to shepherd her return.

She wandered dazed and aimless
drinking in horizons
that offered vague salvation
afraid to take
decisive steps
        for fear she'd be mistaken.

"A burning bush!"
"A cooing dove!"
"A golden ring!"
        she cried,
"I'm lost and need a sign."

The universe stayed silent.

Risk

We anticipate each birth with joy
though we know not every birth
brings a live and undiminished child
    Nearly every one
    is enough
    for hope.
We celebrate each pair who wed
knowing that half who marry
grow disenchanted, break apart
    Still, half becomes
    quite enough
    to risk.
We endure death's coming to others
but deny our own end to life
though no one lives forever
    We simply proceed
    as though
    we will.

jan bohall

My writing life is studying and working in an ongoing poetry workshop during half of each year, and wrestling words into poems on my own the other half. Writing fits into and around my living; I try to put down drafts of poems scrawled in longhand at least five days a week, then revise on the computer. I have placed a poem in *Passager: A Journal of Remembrance and Discovery*, and have won honorable mention in contests in *ByLine* for poems in formal structure, a villanelle, and classic haiku.

jan bohall

Street Heat

Summer
baked-down heat
rising from city street
heat that blazes in eyes
reddens faces, necks, ears, tops of feet
heat that brings gentlewomen in wide-brimmed hats
to leave cooled air behind
emerging, squinted eyes through smoky lenses
as composed as if the day were cool
walking fast on highest heels.
Heat that causes old men to shade themselves
with cast-off newspaper, huddle with friends
at chess or dominoes
under cool Carolina catalpas
heart leaves wilting in afternoon sun
trunk surrounded by sidewalk squares.
Smells of sweat
spattered grease
food cooked with windows open
to catch a nonexistent breeze.
Children with bare feet
trying not to wince, no sign of weakness
as they skim hot coals of sidewalk
break open a hydrant
to ease the shimmering heat
and splash for a few moments
edged out by larger children, larger feet.
Baked-down heat of city street
in summer.

November

Brave November,
I have heard your chariot
of wind echo in the North sky,
riding over the last gold days
of October.

Birth month of winter,
whisper once again your name
among autumn's undressing trees—
their fading faces fall before
young souls age.

Hide me safely,
beneath your leaf-shattered
cape. Sing to me the pilgrims'
prayer of harvest time when simple
hearts gathered.

Hold me close,
as smoke-dimmed dreams of
summer flee and ice slips upon an
unsuspecting sea—I need
your valiant stars.

Stay with me,
until December comes
to sweep your spare hills white,
until your dying breath kisses
the last rose goodbye.

Barbara Brady

(b. 1944, Washington, D.C.), is a poet and artist joyously seeking the "tenth muse" amongst the woods, fields and waves of Edwardsville, Virginia. Her poetic offerings have appeared in several academic and regional publications, including the 1997 volume of *The Poet's Domain*.

Barbara Brady

The Last Voyage

Arise my friend, it's dawn.
Step lightly in her shadow,
sweet memories will follow,
company for the voyage.

Your watch bell rings octet;
safe harbors keep safe ships.
But you have journeys windward,
beyond the fleet-bound port.

Old patriots dream young—
wake them gently. Fearless
hearts together beat as one,
whisper your good-byes.

Flags of glories past soar,
to greet the breaking morn.
Salute them as they rise,
wise from battles won.

It is time. The eagle calls
"serviam" no more beneath
the silver sky. Seeking
wisdom in the clouds, he flies.

Lift your steadfast anchor,
and gracefully slip away.
Sail on, my friend, farewell!
Don't keep tomorrow waiting.

The Road I Took

The road I talked about traveling
When I was nine years old
Was a country road with a cottage home
I shared with a husband and children.
The reality I foresaw
Was a funeral march.
I was a beautiful corpse in my Sunday best
Laid to rest before I could grow old alone.
A child isn't supposed to think like that.
But I took neither road.
I chose poetry.
I made use of my life sentence.
I wrote.
I wrote of other people's weddings and grave sites.
I wrote love songs to other people's children.
I wrote as I walked down my road
An endless, winding road where anything
can happen.
And because I chose to be revived
With the stroke of a simple pen
My road becomes a kingdom.

Ann Catherine Braxton

was born in Charlottesville, Va. and is a thirty-year resident of Hampton, Va. She works as a mental health professional with the Hampton-Newport News Community Services Board. She has harbored a burning passion for poetry since age seven and says she is inspired by the biblical Psalms, the voices of Romantic and Victorian lyricists, and the modern language of ordinary, common folk.

Ann Catherine Braxton

Charlottesville Mountain Miracle

I wanted to touch the mountain trees
To hold them in my fingertips
To freeze their exquisite hue in a mere snapshot
Such folly! What camera can approach
Fog that kisses the mountaintops
Rests on regal evergreens
And flirts with a timid sun peering through?
Hail the Great Painter who knew best!
He granted his living clay a treasure
That cannot be manufactured
Loveliness that lives in grateful eyes
And the sunlight of the soul.

Birthday

Our time is golden in the fading day
As thoughtfully we dream and reminisce.
We may seem to others old and gray,
But we are living moments of quiet bliss
Unblemished, unconcerned by mounting years,
So precious now to cherish and to keep.
Our yesterdays have paid the toll of tears
The harvest of our lives today we reap.

Come let us walk along the sandy shore
And breathe the tingling freshness of the air,
Give thanks for this and hope for one day more
The crystal beauty of our love to share.
Let us be joyful, let us laugh and sing!
Age has no meaning in eternal spring.

Sheila Cardano

A native of England, she has resided on the Eastern Shore of Virginia since 1989. Her poetry has been published in almost all the volumes of *The Poet's Domain*. Her original plays are regularly presented by Arts Enter at the Palace Theatre, Cape Charles, Va. She teaches drama and directs the plays in this non-profit organization.

Seagull

A seagull hovering on the water,
Watching keenly for her prey,
Gliding swiftly in wide circles—
Hunting at the close of day.

Seems to be the wings of angels
Glinting in the sinking sun!
What a splendid sight, a seagull—
Fishing, when the day is done.

Suddenly, the light is ended.
Lovely seagull disappears.
I wonder why my heart is aching,
And my eyes are full of tears.

Requiem for Janie

No more will Janie tread our sun-filled room,
With upright carriage and lithe, sure-footed grace.
Our quiet household heavy now with gloom,
And our memory of her ways we'll n'ere efface.

No more the steady, knowing looks she gave,
As though omnisciently she viewed the scene.
But now she lies safely in the grave,
'Neath trees and shrubs she loved, and cover green.

Can any creature fill the void, her place,
Or replicate the character she displayed?
Can any another creature match her grace,
Her loving ways time and time replayed?

This Maine coon cat was special in her way;
We will not see her like for many a day!

Allan Chase

(b. 1916, New York, N.Y.) graduate of the City College of New York. He spent twenty-eight years working world-wide as a Foreign Service officer in the U.S. Department of State, retiring in 1976 with the permanent diplomatic title of First Secretary and Consul, Retired. He has been writing rhyming verse since 1978, has been published in volumes 14 and 17 of *The Poet's Domain* and participates actively in the poetry proceedings of several groups in the Reston, Va. area. He is a resident of Reston and Chincoteague, Va.

Allan Chase

Thoughts at Dawn

Night's passage breeds incremental change,
A matter only Nature can arrange.

But incremental change is not discrete:
Day evolves from night, an imperceptible feat.

Our sleep is sandwiched between the night
 and day,
While mysterious nether dreams have room to play.

Each dream an evanescent state impure,
Its meaning insubstantial, quite unsure.

But from dream-ridden night a bright day
 emerges free,
A *tabula rasa* of promise for you and me.

Leslie Clark

who was born and raised in New Jersey, lived and taught in Virginia for more than twenty years. She earned her M.A. in English through the creative writing program at Old Dominion University in 1991. Her poetry and short fiction have been widely published for more than twenty years. She and her husband live in Cochise County, Arizona, where Leslie coordinates and participates in many writers' activities. She is also editor/publisher of a monthly online poetry journal, *Voices on the Wind.* http://personalriverusers.com/~geclark/

Flowerings

My mother's New Jersey garden was sentenced
to a linear life.
Up against the fence line, like a row of prisoners,
stood
the tulips, daffodils, hyacinths—disciplined
bulb blooms
of early spring, no straying onto the sparse
green lawn
for them or for their companion bushes. A
spindly rose
or two, some stunted azaleas, the faint yellow
hope of forsythia.
After such restraint, her own riotous late
blooming was inevitable.

Gardens in Virginia were domineering, their
azaleas
bearing no resemblance to those of cooler
climes—aggressive,
overblown lusciousness of fuchsia, flushing
pink, branches scratching
at brick walls of houses, bullying one another
for garden space.
Summers ripe and rank with gaudy greenery,
the jungle growth of every
flower, the tangled mass of weeds, grass that
demanded
the daily songs of mowers. In such a setting,
humans pale.

High desert flowers conceal themselves among
tall grasses,
must be searched for to be seen—delicate violet
and gold stars.

Leslie Clark

One must step gingerly, eyes to ground to
avoid the trampling of such tenderness.
Sheets of poppy gold and blue lupine stalks
    that rival the sky in shadings
Emerge only after winters with rare, generous rain.
The flowers of drier summers are girded with
    other-worldly thorns, daring
desert dwellers to attempt to harvest moisture
    from them.
Here, nothing's given free.

Teaching Poetry

The arrogance of thinking that it can be taught
like a word problem in math.
If X uses Y metaphors for Z number of years,
how many air miles must the resulting product
travel before some self-important editor deigns
to publish it in a magazine read by
perhaps twenty other poets?

What is it that we teach?
That we must scoop to the very bottom
of emotional cartons to extract
the most bitter sweetness.
That there is magic in metaphorical messages,
soothing sibilance, alliterative angst.
That at least once a week, every poet reads
someone else's work, so masterful
that she despairs over her own shallow efforts.

That she keeps writing anyway because she must.
That poets must support themselves
by doing something else.
That revision is never finished.
That we write. We write. We write.

The Superiority of Women!

Janet is a real sweet and most pretty mental
health social worker who powerfully lifts barbells
and dumbbells to keep her health at a peak.
Being with some male patients at work who are
bigger and stronger who grow unruly, she takes
"judo" for "super self-defense" twice a week.

Having style, wit, grace, and ingenuity during
social occasions she's always a superb host.
Also, men enjoy seeing her huge and round bottom
openly wiggle when it really shows the most!

She's quite a gal considering she's a good female
judoist, an excellent therapist, and a loving bride.
Her professionalism outshines most men due to her
feminine charm, and she always offers it with pride!

Jonny Cochran

I've been writing for a awhile. I've had a lot of my literary work published. I also had a picture I took printed in a nationally distributed magazine. I like nature, traveling, sports, socializing, being consistently diligent, and many other things. This is my first appearance in *The Poet's Domain.*

Risking a Life

(Written after reading *The Horse Dealer's Daughter*
by D.H. Lawrence)

Afraid of my own
cold grave reflection,
I simply walked
into the water

not to be reborn
but to wash the dark spots
from my body,
pale, already dead.

When I knew
I had finally
made one single
life-decision,

there you were, gasping
pretending to save me.
Now that you used me
to save yourself,

What do we do with
our sudden
oneness,
our nakedness?

Shirley F. Cox

(Born in Grundy, Va.) recently retired after teaching English, drama, and creative writing at Randolph-Henry High School and at Southside Community College. Her poetry, which has won prizes in both Virginia and Ohio Poetry Society contests, has been published in *Poetry Motel* and the Poetry Society of Virginia *Anthology of Poems*. An avid golfer, she lives in Farmville, Va. This is her fifth appearance in *The Poet's Domain*.

Shirley F. Cox

Dirty Linen

The best thing about living on this hill
was stringing up my wash so all could see
mine was the whitest. Wouldn't have pastel
sheets. I never missed a Monday; thirty
years up at four, a fire in the backyard,
filled the tub from the spring, put in the lye,
boiled my whites in the same tub as the lard,
washed in the Maytag, on the line by five.
Some Mondays even if the clothes were clean
I washed them anyway to let people know
just because Dave had left me did not mean
I no longer believed in the motto
that the most important is cleanliness.
Yes, right up there along with godliness.

Cutting Out Your Own Tonsils

(Described by girl on talk show)

You took cuticle scissors, exacto knife
and in front of the bathroom mirror,
you whittled away little pieces
day by day, until after four months
you had performed your own tonsillectomy.

The reason, you say, was that
you couldn't afford to pay someone
to ease your pain, your recurring
infections. The penicillin cost too much.
Your hoarse voice gives your story
a certain sovereignty, forlornness.

It sounds so easy I'm pondering my own
self-surgery. Every day I tell my
reflection: today is the day I snip
him from my heart, for I too
can't afford recurring infections.

Tornado Game

Gusts grabbed our long hair,
whirled our skirts,
sent us spinning.
Arms outstretched, heads back, we chanted
 tornado,
sang monster movie tunes, drew out the vowels
 —ooh aah.
Wind
sent our dolls skittering
paper cups tap tapping across the drive
and we dashed in and out of the picnic table legs
to grab them.

Off in the distance lightning bolts speared
the chunky sky,
magic
raised the hair on our necks.
The flash of cold air raised goose bumps on
our bare arms.
We twirled our dolls and watched the sky
churn pea green on black.
Dad, in his white golf shirt, watched from the
back steps
and we begged for one last game
above the howl.
His voice, deep and calm, cut through the whir,
and we trudged in the house, shoulders slumped.

We lined up our dolls on the cement pantry floor,
studied our pink wristwatches,
wondered if the tomato soup cans would fall
 on our heads.
Dad stood sentry by the too-short door
and we listened to the sirens and our heartbeats.

Terry Cox-Joseph

(b.1957, St. Paul, Minn.) is an artist, author, and editor, freelancing from her home in Newport News, Va. She is a former newspaper reporter and editor, and has had one book of nonfiction published, *Adjustments*, 1993, and is working on a novel, called *Barren*. She is the coordinator for the annual Christopher Newport University Writers' Conference and contest.

Terry Cox-Joseph

There Were Seven

Ode to *Columbia*, February 1, 2003

So many times I have rushed down the stairs
out the door
across the drive,
first to grab
the morning paper,
dance into the kitchen,
flaunt front page headlines four inches high:
gossip, celebrity photos,
Olympic gold medals, politicians' peccadilloes
so I could beat you to the table before your
coffee was brewed.

Today my steps were measured,
for I already knew what was there,
saw the graphics on the Internet,
read from lips of TV broadcasters too young,
stared at smoky images replayed in sickening
sequence
that opened wounds I thought had healed.
Protective tiles failed to insulate
our emotions here on land.
Flames scorched our dreams
and together we watched sugar crystals fall
from the spoon
like ashes to Earth.

Some primal urge remained.
I craved the touch of dry, white pulp,
the smell of ink mingled with your coffee,
the sound of crinkling,
the cadence of routine
because
as I spread the pages on the table
and stared at block letters slammed across the top,
it somehow made it real.

Terry Cox-Joseph

Continuum

They say the house wrens disappeared
when the first gust of cold wind
mixed dancing leaves and snow
into landlocked funnels.
But I never noticed.
I thought they were always here.
I thought I could hear them,
their high pitched refrains,
the essence of children's music boxes
disappearing beneath the eaves,
rising up to
cloudless blue heavens.

When they returned, it was as though
they'd never left

just as I never noticed
when you pulled the door closed behind you.

Suburban Casualty

In the aisle between dairy and orange juice
we greeted one another over shopping carts.
"How was the first day of school?"
Idle banter, chatter, pleasantries, steady,
steady

but my friend concealed news
—a bomb hidden in a yogurt tub—
inescapable.

"It was stressful for my kids," she said.
"Did you know her?"
Suburban housewife, gorgeous house,

chandelier glittering over two story foyer,
pool in back, dogs barking out front.
I frowned, tried to recall.

"She had a fight with her husband,"
my friend lured me into a story of my own life,
"and one of the kids stepped between them."
I frowned again, stepped closer. Shoppers
passed by,
metallic blurs clicked on linoleum.
. . . She went to slap him, missed, struck the
child instead.
Her husband, a lawyer, threatened—
child abuse suit. Next day,
she dropped her kids off at school, drove home,
and hanged herself.

The cold handle of the shopping cart supported me.
Balance. Steady.
The floor had disappeared.
The shelves of cheerfully packaged juices spun.
The voice of my friend receded behind a
bright light and an aluminum shelf.
Steady.

I focus on our perfectly packaged
lives
and watch them come apart at the seams,
leak slowly from the corners like juice in a
paper container,
or explode on the floor like glass containers of
olives.

Her newsprint face lures me like a siren.
She was A Perfect Person.
She smiled.
Smiled and kissed them goodbye.

Steady,

steady.

Still Falls the Rain

Still falls the rain on the town as it dreams.
While bright neon signs spill their bold
rainbow traces,
the feet of the wandering splash sidewalk streams.

The lone and the lonely find peace in the seams
of the night where their eyes are not forced to
meet gazes.
Still fall the eyes and the town, of them, dreams.

To those who are drowning how gray the dawn
seems;
a sky dressed in downpour no daybreak embraces.
The feet of the sunrise flee light on fresh streams.

Though cloud cohorts hide the high sun and
its steam
stains the air with a smoked haze that lazes,
still falls the rain on the town in its dreams.

Up-flowering umbrellas bloom in the streets.
The chill showering water scrubs exposed faces.
The feet of the school children splash sidewalk
streams.

Caught in the mirroring raindrops that gleam
on the windows, the houses seem much smaller
places.
Still falls the rain on the town in my dreams;
looking back makes no track in the smooth
sidewalk streams.

Elaine Cramer

(b. 1953, Baltimore, Md.) graduated from Drew University with a degree in Anthropology. As a systems analyst, Elaine spent many years writing computer programs but has traded her lines of 'code' for verse. She resides in Hartly, Del., with a cat and itinerant hummingbirds. Three of her poems appeared in *The Poet 's Domain*, volume 19.

Elaine Cramer

Exeunt Omnes

the choral voice in its fullness,
chorded and thick with complements,
sweeps out the music room window.
stately, its sinuous progress
ripples the heads of peonies
scattering sweet scent and petals.

notes glisten on grass the hired man mows.
a robin stops mid-hop and tips his head.
while melody swells round him,
his oval body rides its rising surge
then drops to foraging again.
down the lane, onto the trafficked street it flows
merging with the murmur of engines,
the idling drivers.

its rhythm buoys the feet of the jogger,
and lifts the ends of the jogger's lips.
across the littered road it rolls,
lapping at buildings, peering in windows.
the choral whisper washes
the face of the hospital,
but the sick and the grieving,
the newborn and leaving encased therein
cannot not hear its soothing harmonies.

it stammers on in a widening, weakening wave.
a passing freight train catches some loose notes
and spirits them away.

There's Music in My Kitchen!

There's music in my kitchen!
It's not that it hasn't been there before. . . .
The tunes are even nicer now and I enjoy
them so much more!
My percolator makes surging crescendos as the
fresh, awakening aroma sings to my senses. . . .
While in my laundry room my Kenmore
responds to a firm finger finding and the only
agitation I feel
is the happy vibration of the churning as it
rotates active golf shirts, stretched slacks, and
favorite underpinnings.
. . . and by my sink, a melodious hum splashes watery, steamy melodies in thirty-six year
old hand-washed dishes.
. . . another kind of Kenmore . . . in my
kitchen . . . my dishes . . . sparkly, shiny clean . . .
after thirty six years . . . an automatic dish-
washing machine!
Ah! Three soft notes remind me that the
bacon in the microwave is ready. . . .
And now that it's finished, I can make toast in
the little oven without blowing a fuse . . .
unless of course
The counterpoint in the refrigerator's heart
Intercepts and leaves my kitchen in darkness.
. . . suddenly . . . in high G# (a penetrating key)
the smoke alarm alerts me to my toast
. . . and the scraping percussive process in the
sink, creating
charcoaled crumbs, offers no alternatives for
the only bread!
Music! Exciting measures! Mechanical, elec-
trifying interludes of sound . . .
reassuring me . . . that
after 82 years . . . it's nice to be around!

Barbara McCreary Crann

(b. 1921, Evanston, Ill.) has written poetry since childhood. She attended Northwestern University's School of Speech and the Universities of Hawaii and Virginia. Currently she is completing an autobiography detailing her early battle with mental illness and pioneering use of shock therapy in the late 30s. She resides in Alexandria, Va. with her husband. She served as president of the Alexandria branch of the National League of American Pen Women from 1995–1998.

Barbara McCreary Crann

Lady

What do you think as you sit there alone,
Crouched in that doorway? Is it your own?
Week after week I see your blank stare.
Do you have family? Why are you there?
What do you have in those three shopping bags?
Is it hand-me-down clothing or old cleaning rags?
Are you waiting for someone . . . maybe a bus . . .
To help you escape from life's clutter and fuss?
What do you read in the paper you hold?
Is it news of today or news that's grown old?
Does it tell you of riots and car wrecks and rape
And ravaging storms . . . or the president's shape?
Do headlines confuse? Can you see? Can you read?
Can you hear King Street traffic? What do you heed?
Why are you bundled in cold weather gear
When the day is so warm and the summer so near?
. . . Perhaps you are happier, lady, than some
Who have money to spare and children to come
To visit or comfort . . . Hey, lady, there,
What are you thinking? Does anyone care?

He Makes the Morning Darkness, He Treads on the Heights of the Earth

B. R. Culbertson

(b. 1929, Lynchburg, Va.) is a conjugal facilitator living in Blacksburg, Virginia. Her work has appeared in several volumes of *The Poet's Domain*, as well as *The Lyric*, *Southern Poetry Review*, *The Comstock Review*, *Passager*, *The Sow's Ear*, *Potpourri*, *Blue Unicorn*, and elsewhere.

With what temerity we argue
that God could not have done His job
in seven days . . . and then we swallow
whole: mythology as if it were multiplication,
accepted, provable—how the micro-
biologist walks the paths of DNA
beneath his scope. What idiots
we show ourselves, top heavy
with facts, as unable to stand
as a bug on its back.

The times we leave our lonely dance
long enough to admit He has us pegged
—a little lower than the angels—
that's when the particles collide,
invite new possibilities. We get to watch
stars born.

The thing is balance. Wrapped
in concentric circles we'll fall in.
Society's more circular
than linear; interconnectedness
requires life's curves.
We may feel trapped in never-ending
orbit, hemmed in, enfolded,
smothered, belted-in . . .

But there: amid the crackle of stars—
angels watching, searching
for a place to land!

B. R. Culbertson

Odysseus Landlocked

They are land-caught in the cove;
not trapped . . . but safe, like a boat at last
in harbor. Soft mountains rise

in ranks above the meadow flats.
Sea lover, he catches the wind
in his nostrils as it blows across the sea

of grass. A sentinel pine at the edge
of the field is the mast of a ship
on the horizon of their world.

They camp for the night on the cold ground,
crackle of stars above. Body warms
body, wrapped in down. Silent
the owl floats across the stars.
Nearby the rabbit, the vole
hold quiet and still.

In the morning, his breath
is frost in his hair. He watches her
like the sailor his woman

after a year at sea.

B. R. Culbertson

Facing the Facts

The moon's what saves the city—(sorry place!)
Sunshine exposes too much grit and dirt;
trash lies in heaps, blows by, flies in your face.
Your tolerance grows short; your senses hurt.
You simply cannot see the stars, when bound
within a city's streets. The lights that glow
shine on both deeds and perpetrators found,
but steal star sheen for streetlights' lurid show.

I'd like to trade the office for a farm,
and overlook sad fact: I'm ignorant
of how they do it! I might wreak much harm
on land and stock, no matter my intent.

No—I'll stay here, let moonlight fill my dreams,
until, moon-washed, the dirty city gleams.

Coffee at the End of the Millennium

I once drank coffee black, avoiding guilt
of sugar and the calories of cream;
felt virtuous, stayed working at full tilt
when lazier types had gone to sleep, to dream.
Coffee the treasured starter of my days,
good keeper of my temper and my muse. . . .
I had become complacent in my ways,
dependent on the drug I chose to use.
Now shade-grown coffee's sheltering trees are cut;
chemicals and sun speed growth—and cost,
while migratory songbirds' routes are shut—
they search in vain for sanctuary lost.
No more the flitting gems, sun glint in rain—
nor do I enjoy my coffee without pain.

Eden's Lost Music

O sing thou fairest bird
of Paradise
for cherished is your
vibrant melody—
Extol enticing notes of
Love's virtues—
while your golden wings
fan gracefully
weaving ardent tones
of majestic tapestry
with Dawn's unerring streams
of light—

But your sweet song fades
and disappears
and the deep soul of earth
is forged with tears—
Though they may fashion flowers
for Summer's mirth
they splash in mourning like
tattered cherry blossoms.
For Paradise cast out her
singing bird
and Silence dwells where music
once was heard—

Josephine Darner

(b. 1928, Washington, D.C.) has worked in the theater as both dancer and actress and still enjoys taking dance classes. This is the eighth appearance of her poetry in *The Poet's Domain*. ROAD Publishers has published two of her books of poetry, *The Music of Memories* in 1995, and *The Dance Within* in 1999. Ms. Darner is a member of The National League of American Pen Women, where she serves as Vice President of the Bethesda Chapter. She lives in Rockville, Md. where she continues to write poetry and also likes to participate in local poetry readings.

Josephine Darner

Uncle Willie

Each day he sat in the same rocking chair
on the edge of the long grey porch—
He rocked gazing out over the humming orchard
grazing in the meadows of recall—

His body was gaunt and he dressed in an old
black suit—
on his head of brushed white hair
he wore a grey fedora or a panama of faded
straw—
Both weathering years of Wednesday evening
prayer meetings,
Both tipped at myriad, mournful, small-town
funerals—
His face was ever thin and somber—
Tight-lipped he rarely spoke that I remember—

While I ran and laughed and played and swung
holding fast to the ropes of the tire-swing
arcing high
in the branches of the giant tulip poplars
Uncle Willie painted in the shadowy cave of
his log cabin—

He painted landscapes with rivers and trees—
Once I peeked in and saw a large canvas
rendering the
ominous image of the Natural Tunnel of
Virginia—
The picture was perfect but the room was small
and dark hardly compatible with the needs of
an artist—

Josephine Darner

Who was this strange great uncle of mine
drifting to and from the big grey house
like a phantom wandering through graves,
leaving for awhile his treasured canvasses
to rock on those summer days
gazing out over the humming orchard
grazing in the meadows of his dreams—

Paths

What thoughts are renegade in the
valleys of the brain?
What broodings hide within the wasteland
of the mind?
What imaginings engage
the vision?
What lies behind the glow
of eye?

What force of will
What sense of soul
lifts one hand
with hate to kill,
the other to
embrace with love?

In that winding maze
I sense that there might
be vestiges of
memories; lost trails
leading to Shangri-La—

Happiness

Happiness is a stranger to me,
A vision most wondrous my eyes cannot see.
A lover's caresses are most alien to me,
A marvelous pain of which I am free.
Happiness is a stranger to me.

Is happiness a law of physics, a Maxwell equation?
A law of nature, evolved by Darwin?
Maybe Murphy's Law defines it,
Uncertain, says Heisenberg.
Happiness is clearly a stranger to me.

I search the heavens for the answer.
But my vision is distorted, just like the Hubble.
I search amongst atoms and molecules,
But the Brownian motion makes me see double.
Happiness is even stranger to me.

Metaphorical hyperbole;
Does happiness resemble thee?
There is no Jackie, Gloria, or Di,
Not even Nancy, Patricia, or Chi.
So maybe happiness is just a dog named Sue.

Spring into Summer

Water puddles in the fields,
Daffodils flowering,
Sap running in the old maple tree,
Robins hopping,
Bluebirds chirping,
Geese nesting,
Ducks testing the ponds!
Harbingers of a new season
Even if the snow is blowing.

Stanley K. Dickinson

(b. 1931, Clarksburg, W. Va.), a geologist retired from Federal service, made his debut in *A Little Nonsense,* and was also published in volumes 15 and 17 of *The Poet's Domain.* He earned B.S. and M.S. degrees in geology at West Virginia University and a Ph.D. at Harvard University. He currently resides in Charles Town, W.Va.

Stanley K. Dickinson

Virginia Lonely

Shenandoah River, Chesapeake Bay,
Blue Ridge Mountain are beautiful today.
If you can't stand the loneliness
You must visit them again some day.

As you search for some other place
You wander to and fro in space.
But it's just Virginia loneliness
That you know is there to face.

Sunsets come and full moons go,
Stars and comets put on a show.
How Virginia lonely they make you feel
As you watch them from below.

So, what more is there to say,
How high the price will you pay?
Make Virginia loneliness go away
Do not live with it each day.

Off into the sunset you may sail
Somewhere out beyond the pale;
But a lonely Virginia will call to you
And beckon you finally home to stay.

Katherine Mansfield

Yes, these were among her perfect gems -
"Prelude," "At the Bay," "Je ne parle pas
Français,"
All created on feverish afternoons
In tubercular exile on the Côte D'Azur
Or in the shabby damp of London flats.
Then, her invalid's world looted and lost,
Death invaded her thirty-sixth year
And genius was hers no more.

Isota Tucker Epes

was born in Norfolk, Va. in 1918, grew up in Pittsburgh, Pa., and graduated from Bryn Mawr College in 1940. Her first job was as an editor in New York; but she left to become a research analyst for O.S.S. in Washington, D.C. during WWII. She and her lawyer husband had four children, and moved to Philadelphia in 1953. At first, Isota held a second editorial job at Bryn Mawr College until she became a teacher of English and then headmistress of The Shipley School. Since retirement, she has been involved chiefly in studying and making art.

Growing Old Gets Simpler and Simpler

Such rot has been written over the years
About the process of growing old—
So many lies, such slippery deceit.
But what is the truth we find at the end?
Simply this, my friend, and nothing better:
One by one, humans struggle to live
Just one more week or one more day,
And, with no subtle aims or complex goals,
To fend off the strangled silence of death
Just one more hour, one more second, one
more breath.

Wealthy American

As a wealthy American
I am both very generous and very stingy
It's very clear when
I jiggle my body—
The tissue and fluids that
Want and love
The movement and
The tissues and fluid that
Get v-e-r-y t-i-r-e-d
And j-u-s-t w-a-n-t t-o h-o-l-d o-n.

To fear this body
Imprisons our freedom
Is an error.

Our life sentence in
This precious human body
Is the pressure cooker.
That is freedom.

Quick, the time to cook
Is short.

Janet Evergreen

(b. 1956) first lived at 4 Pig Rock Lane, Marblehead, Mass. Her spiritual path is supported by Tibetan Buddhist Drikung Kagyu practice and her main deity is pig-headed Vajrayogini. Her work is to be a spiritual friend and guide mainly through cranialsacral manipulation and body centered spiritual processing. Other adventures not foreseen by her birthplace are: she raised one biological daughter, two adopted sons, and dozens of foster kids before discovering her own inner child of luminous light who simply enjoys life in Charlottesville, Virginia.

Listening and Knowing

The drip of snow
Spring is coming
Quiet in the rice pot
The rice is done
Water pouring into the tub
A deeper resonant
Come, get in

Janet Evergreen

Not Too Old

You are not too old
Or too grown up
To be excitement
Like a class 4 rapids
Or to allow yourself
To be flatness
Like a man-made lake
In a park.
No. Self moves through
Either when there is no
Grasping or aversion.
But beware, Self can
Get caught and drown
Or bore itself to death.

Meditation

Delight
Vast, delicious, contagious joy
Disgust
Deadly, dysfunctional, inheritance
My shame is that I passed
On disgust where I could have
Shared delight
It's not too late.

Detest and eyes narrow like a snake
Desire and tentacles go out like an Octopus
Detest pushes desire back down
Desire jumps up like a Jack-in-the-box

Apply the antidote
Pause for the transformation
And what have you got?
Discriminating wisdom and the
Power to do more prostrations.

Clarity and grace to benefit more
Than myself.

Our Dance

The music was dreamy,
The lyrics were tender,
As we swayed to the beat
Of the dance we shared that night.
    The warmth of your nearness,
    The rhythm and motion,
    Gave a magical glow
    To the dance we shared that night.
I'll always remember
That sense of surrender,
Those few precious moments
Of the dance we shared that night.

Joseph Fulton

(b. 1920, Newark, N.J.), an economist retired from the U.S. Library of Congress, graduated from New York University. He has written poetry since high school. This is his sixth appearance in *The Poet's Domain*. He is a member of The Poetry Society of Virginia and has been associated with the poetry workshop at George Mason University. He lives in Annandale Va.

Great Decisions

The first car I bought was an Edsel:
its famous front grill sold me.
My next car was a Yugo:
it was on sale
and came already assembled.
When I worked as a tour guide
I took a group to Mount St. Helens
the day it erupted.
Later I led a flock of tourists
to the Ukraine in time
for the Chernobyl radioactive shower.
Now I'm excited about
my new career as a stockbroker,
where I advise clients on stocks to buy.
May I have your business?

Joseph Fulton

Perception

I read it in a comic strip of all places
"Perception is Reality!"
Ah so?
One can change reality
by changing one's perception of it?
Neat!
So much easier than flying to faraway places
for that new look.

Grampa Joseph

You seem ancient, Grampa Joseph,
Sitting quiet in your chair,
Hair so gray and face so weathered,
Witness to life's wear and tear.
    You have seen much on your journey,
    Happiness and times of pain,
    Have they guided you to wisdom?
    Would you do the same again?
Let me sit here on this footstool,
I am callow, shallow, new,
Let each gray hair teach a lesson,
Help me be the best of you!

Joseph Fulton

Talent

Talent
Some overflow with it,
Gaining fame and fortune,
Bing Crosby, Michael Jordan, Tiger Woods.
    Others have more modest talents
    Best pie at the church social,
    Highest score in the bowling league,
    Getting published in the little journals.
Then there are those without talent,
other than accepting who they are as they are,
and snuggling down comfy cozy,
enjoying the talent of others.

We All Have Poetry

Everyone has poetry.
It's born when we are born.
It's the rhythm of our breathing.
The change from night to morn.

Everyone has rhythm.
Though some have a different beat.
It's in our shouted laughter.
The tattoo of walking feet.

Everyone has poetry.
It comes from living life.
The sounds of joy and sadness,
Of happiness and strife.

There is no one right poetry.
We each have our own kind.
From flowing free-form verse
To classic metered rhyme.

So if you would make poetry,
You need not look too far.
It's how you feel. It's what you do.
And the twinkling of a star.

Nancy R. Furr

(b. 1953, Bainbridge, Ga.) graduated from Virginia Tech with a B.A. degree in elementary education. She resides in Blacksburg, Va. with her husband and two teenage children. She currently works as an aide in the Montgomery County public school system.

Iris

In my garden
Row on row
Iridescent
Scepters grow.

The Strong Voice of Summer

I wake up tasting cigarettes, though I quit
In May, and take the wheel, pulling the night
Toward me as you fall off to sleep.

I have slept just enough to make me tired.
You settle down with the dusky edges
Of night clouds and I envy you.

We are winding out of weekend and day
Travelers, the road ours as much as
Heat lightning over the plains
allows me to believe it.

It rained the first day, a sudden torrent
Manifested from the humidity and resolute
Midwestern lull. We got near Chicago
When we had to stop an hour before we could
Make out sky from land and continue.

All the while your silence sought to devour me,
Your words when they came, convoluted by
Torturous, ethereal smoke dissolving into the
Expanding territory between us. I replied wistfully,
Speaking of rivers flowing inexorably into seas,
As if I could make them right for this scene.

Matthew Genson

(b. 1973) was born and raised in Michigan. After receiving his B.A. in English from Western Michigan University in Kalamazoo, he moved to Virginia where he has worked as a special events planner, a bookstore clerk, and a copywriter for a publishing company. At present, he lives in Palmyra, Virginia with his wife and sons. *The Strong Voice of Summer* is his first published piece.

Matthew Genson

Since then, the stillness has reasserted itself,
The miles between towns giving
Themselves over completely to vastness,
The landscape never bothered by
Its lack of expression.

The world has emptied itself again into night, and
You sleep untroubled while the wind carries
A cascade of hair across your timeless face.

I want to be able to remember this instant,
The stars standing vigilant above our heads,
As the widening orbits of our lives diverge at last.

I pull over to put the top up and switch the radio,
Trying to conjure a memory of a world I've lost
Even as I'm losing this one. As a boy in my room,
When I would sleep to the radio—
Call-in advice shows, AM pop, network news
Breaks at the top of every hour—
Playing over the airwaves like the voice of truth,
At 2 a.m. connoting a world
I could imagine existed, and
Would wait for me to find it.

Beverly Harner

(b.1948, Waynesboro, Va.) a former teacher and librarian, is an artist, musician, writer of poetry and short stories, and a massage therapist/body worker living in Charlottesville, Va. with her dog and two cats. Her writing comes from the heart, speaking the unspoken, making the invisible visible, uplifting and clarifying the mundane. Her spiritual poetry has been published in several issues of *The Voice of Clear Light.*

Frost

(Reflections on an early morning walk)

Grass and leaves are crunching, crunching
under my feet.

The frost is so thick, the ground looks white,
as if covered with a light winter's dusting of snow.

Walnuts decorated with lacy ice crystal patterns
transform into festive holiday ornaments.

Dead leaves on trees coated with nature's glitter
shimmer brightly in the first rays
of the morning sun.

Now the grass looks as if it has been strewn
with handfuls of diamonds,
each reflecting a myriad of rainbow patterns.

I reach to gather some diamonds for my pocket,
but they melt,
lost dreams dripping off my palm.
I turn to look, but you've disappeared.
Where did you go?

Beverly Harner

Ode to the Lightning Bug*

Only God
in His infinite
imagination and playfulness
could create
the Lightning Bug—
which speaks
the language of light
to the night,
spreads magic
through the air,
and gives lighthearted
quiet peace
to our summer
nights and evenings.

I remember
warm, clear
starry nights
at my grandparent's farm,
and our running
through grassy fields
capturing you in jars
to make a firefly's
luminescent flashlight.
I loved your
dancing, twinkling lights
connecting those fields
to the stars, and
transforming the tree tops
into miniature heavens.

*This is written in the form of a "Skinny Ode," made popular by Pablo Neruda so that his poems might be published in his friend's newspaper and so fit in its columns.

Beverly Harner

Are you soaring
on air currents
over the river,
as you blink your
Morse code
mating message
first here then there?
Do you dream
of playing in the day
trying to outshine the sun?
Were you the inspiration
to the cave man
who first invented fire?

You remind me
of the blinking
of an owl's eyes,
of sunflowers waving
by the garden fence,
of a bright yellow
VW Bug.
Were you,
the Lightning Bug,
the inspiration
for that, too?

Carport Appalachia

Flatfoot, shuffle dances
Banjo picking
Low singing
Soulful tunes
Hands slap, clapping
On blue-jean thighs
Appalachian melodies
And rhythms.

A gray head low over his guitar,
The honey hair girl blushes—
Her first solo.
Singing in the people's key brings us home.

Columbine
And dew drops
Wild asparagus
Grow in that place
Of shifting winds,
Of unexpected
Stinging cold.

It is Sunday morning, early.
I listen beyond the birds to echoes—
A carport Saturday night.

Heidi Hartwiger

a freelance writer and a ghost storyteller on the Original Candlelight Ghost Tour of Williamsburg, lives in Yorktown, Va. She teaches writing courses for Christopher Newport University's Lifelong Learning Society. Her first book, *A Gift of Herbs*, Down Home Press, 1993, became a 1995 Rodale Book Club selection. Her non-fiction work includes *All Join Hands: The Forgotten Art of Playing With Children*, Down Home Press, 1994; *Keeper of the Stories; A Motivational Guide for Older Beginning Writers*, Parkway Publishing, 2002; *The Secrets of Indian Knob*, Frog Hollow Press, 2001, is her first novel.

Heidi Hartwiger

Bored

Oh good, gray poet,
I think of you
as I grow tired and sick
of hot, sweet tea
and nougats rolled in chocolate
with crushed walnuts;
more bored, I think,
than you
with your learned astronomer.

There is for me
no perfect silence in your stars.
In nature I find no solace.
From dawn to sunset
squabbling blue jays and cardinals plague me.
Scrambling at the feeder,
they challenge juncos and black cap chickadees
for sunflower seeds,
red milo,
and cracked corn.

Wordsworth advises me to go outdoors
with a heart ready to receive,
but I have weeds to pull,
flowers to water.
So, I wear my hat,
fill the watering can
and hope
Candide,
who lives beyond my picket fence,
won't choose this day
to cultivate his garden.

Heidi Hartwiger

Zanesville Women

I sing the songs of my women,
verses from ballads—
Dear Liza, Aunt Rhody,
hymns to the cradle
rocking and crooning.

I come to my garden
in celebration.
Breathing slowly
their scents:

Gardenia, lavender
Honeysuckle and rose.

My mother, her mother,
their mothers before them.

Their tears on my cheeks,
their cycles of blood,
their green eyes and temper.

I am of them.

Wrens pull at dry grasses,
dragonflies spread lacy wings
on sun-drenched rocks,

And I lift my face to the sun,
close my eyes,
press fingers deep
in rich loam;
my palms,
my wrists,
into dark comfort.

Stage-Mother's Daughter

Little swan—
Waiting backstage to go on
White feathered tiara itching your nose
Pink satin *pointe* slippers pinching your toes
Corseted pudge in classical tutu
Why do you dance when you don't have a mind to
You'd rather climb trees and swing by your knees
Catch a fish, go swim, fly a kite in the breeze.

Who are you trying to please?

Amelia K. Heart

aka Kay Hearton, earned bachelor of arts degrees in dance and in English writing at George Mason University, in Fairfax, Va. She taught dance in the Washington, D.C. area for many years. In 1991, she moved to Virginia's Northern Neck. "Semi-retired," she coaches advanced dancers and enjoys spending more time writing poetry and fiction.

Fractals

My world is as I see it
expanding when I learn—
creative evolution—
a fern within a fern!

With plans around the chaos,
beginnings without end,
where Man can be a poet
and God can be a friend.

How clever the conception!
How wonderful to be
among the thinking creatures
predestined to be free!

And all of us together
unfolding with each turn—
infinity in motion,
a fern within a fern.

Barbara McKay Hewin

(b. 1927, New York, N.Y.), poet and homemaker, won a 1st Place award in the Virginia A.A.U.W. poetry contest. Her poems have appeared in volumes 1 through 20 of *The Poet's Domain*, and in *Poetic Voices of America*, Sparrowgrass Poetry Forum, Inc. She is listed in Writers in Virginia and continues writing from her home in Williamsburg, Va.

Evolution.com

Well now—I think, and so must be!
But something new has been combined with me:
I once scanned distant seas with giant eyes
And grabbed a million bites on every rise,
I broached with unmatched power through the waves
and strained the smallest creature through my staves;
across entire oceans I would feed
to fill the constant and relentless need.
One hundred tons of strength from spout to tail
those ancient times ago when I was Whale.

I saw pale satin pillows and old lace,
high ceiling rooms with everything in place,
dim gilded lamps and flower-patterned walls,

and I was pampered center of it all;
whole days were spent devoted to my care,
to lave and preen each whisker, pad and hair—
fastidious and fine I was at that!
Those ancient times ago when I was Cat.

I walked a thousand quiet corridors
where books and files and catalogues were stored
in perfect order, listed and consigned
to save the products of creative mind,
and I was lord of all the marvels there
dispensing all with clarity and care,
a genius in the science and the plan,
those ancient times ago when I was Man.

And now it seems this migrant finds new rest
within a host that surely is the best!
Now suddenly there is to me much more
than all those bits and pieces there before—
call it a conscience, spirit, God's design,
I feel somehow complete now it is mine,
incorporating Man and Cat and Whale
it holds them all and over all prevails!

Thus final evolution may be known
when ancient souls are cased in silicone!

Fairy Dust

There is no such thing as nothing
in this universe of ours,
glowing nebula and galaxies,
planets, asteroids, and stars;
and a mess of unseen matter
fills the rest of it, they say,
where the particles get smaller
and the quantum gets more fey!

Spellbound

William L. Hickey

(b. 1929, Baltimore, Md.) was an information analyst and writer for the National Council on Crime and Delinquency. He does square, round, and Irish ceili dancing. His poems have appeared in the Poetry Society of Virginia's 80th Anniversary *Anthology of Poems* and in volumess. 17, 18, and 19 of *The Poet's Domain*. He lives to dance and write in Virginia Beach, Va.

A word
connects
Tamara
and I.

A good word;
acceptable,
unalarming,
peaceful.

A light word,
not heavy
for either
to bear.

It floats
in the air,
close,
almost visible.

Unsaid,
as yet
undeciphered,
unknown.

Indistinct,
its letters
glide free,
ungrounded.

Spellbound,
I await
its appearance
joyfully.

William L. Hickey

In-House Poet

He wanted
to be a poet,
he also
wanted a house.

He got a mansion,
his own palace,
it was comfortable
and so was he.

What else
had he wanted,
he couldn't remember,
was it poetic justice?

No matter,
he stepped into
his in-house bar
and had a double entendre.

My Joy: Know How I Feel?

I have walked
no hard roads
nor climbed
any mountains.

There is a metro
to Montmartre,
Montparnasse
is street level.

William L. Hickey

My path
chanced few heights,
has had no depths
only green valleys.

Without depths
I've not won
the great JOY
of the mountain top.

The new day
is a joy
without prospect
no goal in view.

My joy:
a degree conferred,
proud parents,
an army discharge,

Paris life,
Irish ground,
placing words,
dancing Tamara.

No, you don't know
how I feel.
It's my walk
and my talk.

Lesson from the Drought

Cherish the past,
live in the present,
look to the future—
Believe that the time right now,
will, in turn, become
the good old days.

Black clouds bring hope,
for what we once thought was bad
is all turned around.

God's *aqua vitae* is
not encased in the glorious sun,
nor in its fabulous
blue backdrop,
but in
grey torrents of
dark
pelting
colorless
tasteless
cold
droplets.

Todd Hubley

(b. 1943, Louisville, Ky.) from Silver Spring, Md. lives an active life as a research interviewer, short story writer, amateur playwright and poet, and is making his sixth appearance in *The Poet's Domain*. In 1998, he qualified as a semifinalist for writing the best poem at the International Society of Poets' annual convention held in Washington, D.C. Other unpublished works include *The Five Mansions of Stone* and *We Only Meet at Funerals*.

Lambs and Lions

Winter yawning in trees
in dawn's crisp air
jonquils, hyacinths
refusing to back down,
red mercury
in see-saw fashion
perking in the spring;
cock robin strutting
in his domain
as brief grass
inches up
around his feet.
Spring trying
to perch on winters' tail,
the race is on—
winter slow to sleep
spring running in.

Nancy Stuart Hundley

(b. 1934 Richmond, Va.) is a member of the Poetry Society of Virginia, has had poems published in the 1985, 1993, and 2003 *Anthology of Poems*. She has had over a dozen poems published in *The Piedmont Literary Review*, Danville, Va. Other works have been published in various journals and magazines. This is her eighth appearance in *The Poet's Domain*. She divides her time between Richmond and Boydton, Va.

Where Does a Poem Come From?

Words with music dancing around one's head
little words, long words waiting to be said
singing words rolling, tumbling
down into valleys of song
across meadows into autumn's array
snug, cozy as flowers in a bouquet.
A poem comes from the high seas
slides onto the shore
into sea shells on the sand—
poems come from tops of trees
sliding down slender bending limbs
blowing into a gentle breeze
across yards to bending knees.

St. Patrick's Day Sunrise

At 6 a.m., hastily wrapped, we step out
for a wider view of incredible colors
interfused and overlying.
What portent lies in this fiery blaze?
Has expected warfare suddenly flamed?

Has bombing started in Iraq?
Bolts of boldness behind the mountain's gap
still us with hypnotic power—with mouths
agape we breathe in air unwarmed
by distant radiance.
Unshivering abelias calmly wait for first
sparkle on lackluster green; hungry azaleas
reach out for their breakfast
of gently warmed morning-glow.
Dampened ground releases drink to folded petals
where yesterday's crocus quilt slowly opened. . . .

Will morning again astound us with lace-trimmed
white, clusters of yellow, curves of purple,
and streams of pastel blue?
Surely St. Patrick's will hasten the greening too,
as surely as the sun that always rises,
as swiftly as the gathering of coalition forces,
as timely as the spring with its promise of hope.
as revealing as the visions of what is to be.

Rosalie S. Jennings

(b. 1917, Woodstock, Va.) is a member of the Valley Branch of Virginia, National League of American Pen Women. She has recently had eight of her poems depicted by an artist and displayed in a local showing. Her 1999 illustrated chapbook *Leaning On Rhythms* has been well received and is on display in local libraries and in the Washington, D.C., League of American Pen Women library.

Rosalie S. Jennings

Right Place for Love

I see you there by the dogwood
looking up thru the creamy-white flow
searching in vain for a cat-injured bird.
You are here by the double window
looking out at our new springtime
watching two robins peering into the yew.
You are there in the rocker, your eyes
dancing sparks at the TV showing
of prisoners waving, coming home from Iraq.

Now, why is there question about your returning?
Isn't our earth "the right place for love?"
My long-ago anger, my grief-filled yearning
have tempered to waiting, to looking ahead
for some new experience to live through with you.
Digging out thistles, pesky old creepers,
test my resentment that I'm now alone,
that it's not your back that bends to the task
but only your presence, your cautions, your
pleasure
that lift me and thank me for diligent vigor.
Frost calls our "earth the right place for love"—
perhaps so in heaven, some far-away realm,
but the clay of creation was made of great need,
of great care and wonder—this I believe!
Of all man's pursuits, of all of his wants,
the greatest is love that is found—and returned.

What I'd Wish For

(the male point of view)

If I were nine—
　　a fishing pole and line
If I were twelve—
　　a baseball glove
If I were fifteen—
　　a car, all mine
If I were eighteen—
　　a girl to love
Now that I'm grown:
　　All of the above!

Barbara Daniels Johnson

(b. 1928, Cleveland, Oh.) has lived in the Alexandria, Va. area since 1934, She has three daughters and one grandson. Interests include church, crafts and children. She is active in scouting, vacation bible school, and senior choir (invited to sing at the White House). She is assistant treasurer, Alexandria Branch, National League of American Pen Women, and a member of its Poetry Workshop. She authored *Shared Happiness*, a book of poetry.

Delecter

Sitting closely, I inhale your aroma. Salivating,
my brain urges me to eat, to devour you.
Ablutions performed, using thumbnail, your
rainbow-tinted flesh is flayed.
Living skin, sun-kissed pink, coral, lavender.

Passively, you submit to your deep, hard core.
Given no succor, you are mine.
Rest in peace.

Your brothers and sisters watch, cringing
before this deadly onslaught. Ha!
Rightfully so.

Now playing high priest, I anoint them with
chrism and viaticum. My silvery
knife flashes, slices. If a scream or confession
arises, none can hear.

Now bagged and tagged, entombed in
A freezing clime, victims of cannibalistic
obsession. Sweet.

Fructus Angelicus! What have you done to
deserve such a fate? Being, being a perfectly
ripe peach.

Maureen Kaczynski

was born in Washington, D.C. in 1934. She published an amusing article in her local paper, *The Daily Press*, concerning her "infamous" surname. Maureen received honorable mention for her poem, *The Beauty and the Benadryl*™, at the Christopher Newport University Writer's Conference. Mother of four, grandmother of six, she aspires to writing short stories presently gestating in her brain. Maureen and her husband, Ted, reside in Hampton, Va.

Maureen Kaczynski

The Beauty and the Benadryl™

Earthworms caress her palms,
ladybugs vie to alight on her seven-year-old flesh.
In her presence, clover seems to grow a fourth
leaf. Lucky.

Spring lays offerings on her enchanted altar,
as though my fey child a goddess.
Sooty-lashed Irish blue eyes wide. She believes.

Now wearing a dandelion woven necklace,
carrying her experiment labeled, "Poysan barries"
in a Dixie™ cup, she is ready for school.
Show and Tell.

But wait, there is more.

Carefully selected shrub and tree leaves,
wrapped in snowy white napkin (my best linen),
tied hobo style on a deadwood stick.
Forgetting to ask, "Mother may I?"

How can I forbid her this? Shhh.

At the pollen-shrouded car, her treasures are
put aside.
Perfect handprints impressed where they will.
She cries with joy,
"Look, its going to be a lime-green day!"

Inserting the car key, I sneeze.

Grandchildren Suite

Continuence

For Greg

A late night call to us in Maine
Our bags were ready for the flight
We drove all day and half the night.

His head mishapen, red and bruised
His tiny toes and fingers curled
A hard time coming to the world.

Triumphant mother, sobered dad
Our children shared the awesome joy
Of welcoming their baby boy.

Something momentous in our lives occurred

Our first grandchild was born today

Immortality assured
For one more generation.

Pat Allen Kaplon

(b. 1936, Eckhart, Md.) resides in Madison, Va. Mrs. Kaplon earned her B.S.Ed. degree at Frostburg University and her M.S. in English education from Towson University, both in Maryland. Mrs. Kaplon is an avid reader of both prose and poetry. She writes in both mediums and has written a book of poetry called *Touchstones*, a novel entitled *A Child Called Hope*, and a children's book called *Betsy's Choice*. Her poetry has won prizes in several national competitions.

Pat Allen Kaplon

Dancer

Megan danced for me
'Round and 'round she twirled,
miming Brittany's look

Pouty lips, flashing eyes,
Swaying hips
Sensuous arms
Moving to the rhythms of her song

So young, yet so intent
on pleasing
Dancing as she saw
her grown up idol do

A lovely, little dancer
enchanted by her dream

Pat Allen Kaplon

Shell Seeker

For Katie

Not so many years ago,
When you were three or four,
We took summer vacation
Together, at the shore.

You feared the unknown ocean,
Thought whales were lurking there,
And so, we walked along the beach
To search for treasures rare.

Each time we spied a seashell,
You'd choose it, without fail.
There was no shell, or part of one
Too small to fit your pail.

We strolled together, hand in hand,
Our sandy beach-way wending,
Immersed within the joy we felt,
Together moments spending.

You may seek sea shells all alone
One day, when we must part—
Then, recall that lovely summer
And hold it in your heart.

Pat Allen Kaplon

Flight School

In the flower garden
On a lovely summer morn
Lindsey and I spoke of dinosaurs

Suddenly, above us,
A bluebird swiftly flew
Circled once, then soared into the sky

Lindsey's eyes were shining
As she turned to me and said
"I wish that I could fly high like that bird."

Looking at her hopeful face
I wondered what to say
Then asked, "Why don't you flap your arms and try?"

Lindsey stepped up on a rock
She spread her arms out wide
She made her body ready for the flight

She flapped and flapped her little arms
Then gave a mighty leap
Fell swiftly through the air and hit the ground

She looked up with a puzzled frown
Brushed off her knees and hands
"It's not working," she complained to me

"Well, maybe you should try once more,"
I suggested with a smile.
Lindsey thought a moment, then agreed.

She climbed up to a higher rock
She flexed her arms and flapped
Then threw herself into the air, but fell

Lindsey got up from the ground
Again and shook her head
"I don't think that I can do it," she exclaimed

She came and sat with me once more
We both looked at the sky.
She sighed, and let her dream of flying die

Lights of Paris

After the Rue de Berri newsroom dims
and presses begin to roll far below,
at last, wishing Boris the driver
bonsoir,
I relax against car cushions
for the nightly ride across the city.
Lamps in narrow cobblestone streets
cut swaths through dark canyons
of the night.
Rows of bright moons light Avenue
Franklin Roosevelt,
and sparklers hang along the Champs
Elysées—
ropes of diamonds on the Pont Alexandre,
fireflies caught in globes in chestnut
trees of Boulevard des Invalides.

Coming into the brazen blaze of Boulevard
        Montparnasse cafés, the car
runs past the bright nightspots
and into the quiet Boulevard Port Royal,
to stop below the single warm yellow
        square of light awaiting me
seven stories above.

Carrie Jackson Karegeannes

(b. 1923, Wusih, China), retired editor and writer for newspapers and three government agencies, has appeared in fourteen volumes of *The Poet's Domain* and in other publications, most recently in the Poetry Society of Virginia's *80th Anniversary Anthology of Member Poets*. She is also a member of the National League of American Pen Women and the Academy of American Poets. She now lives in Falls Church, Va.

Carrie Jackson Karegeannes

Crossing 14th Street Bridge

Rose-salmon light fades above dappled
steel of the Tidal Basin,
faintly rose-touched, ringed with lights.
Sea gulls swirl thick as snowflakes.
Through them, surely almost through them,
surges a jet from National Airport.
And another.
And still the gulls swirl.

The light dims.
Jefferson standing tall and alone
in his greatcoat
gazes across the water from his rotunda
to Washington's luminous shaft.
Crossing the bridge, the bus meshes
into traffic.
Faintly in the distance glows
Lee's mansion,
occasional flicker of Kennedy's Flame
below.

I could not have asked that
for you.
But I could wish—
I could wish the eternal memory
for you.

Carrie Jackson Karegeannes

After 9/11/01

I look up to sliver of moon
serene in night-blue sky
sprinkled with sparks of light.

No—not stars this night:
they move,
criss-crossing all the sky,
guarding the city.

Chance Words

I do not remember the Atlanta streets
        or the tram.
I do not see your mother's house
        or table.
I remember dinner was Chinese,
but I recall scant talk
        of our Shanghai days.

Yet, these years later, chance words—
        "buzz bombs"—
flash back the evening.
Elbows on white porch railing,
we leaned into the dark.
Fresh from war, you spoke
        of London days and nights.

Aragulous June

'Tis malakaridge
To budge not a bwidge,
To frabble away
On Horswagle Bay.

Sail with me
Across the sea,
June, June, Aragulous June,
In my brave little frigatoon.

Others may
Frabble away
Sailing forever
On Horswagle Bay.

But, June, we
Shall sail the sea
And loveabamboom
'Neath smearling moon.

We'll laugh
At bad weather
Just being together
In our brave little frigatoon.

We'll sail far away
From Horswagle Bay
Across the sea
To Nuka Ki.

There, we'll fibble,
Jibble and jig,
Feasting on oyster,
Parrot, and pig,

Robert L. Kelly

A retired shipbuilder, Bob began writing poetry under the mentorship of Christine Sparks in the LifeLong Learning Society at Christopher Newport University. There, he also studied under Mary-Jean Lenhart, and now Patricia Flower Vermillion, who challenged him to write a poem based on new sounds. The result was *Aragulous June*. Bob is happily married, living in Newport News, Va., and has four sons and four grandchildren.

Robert Kelly

Breadfruit, taro,
Papaya, and mango;
And hug and squeeze
'Neath coconut trees.

So come, fantagulous June,
To hibble and ribble
In time to my fiddle
To drink the gluse of the moon,

And sail far away
From Horswagel Bay
Where every month
Is June, June, June!

Homecoming

There she is,
Her big brown eyes
Offering adoration
Acceptance, forgiveness.

She crosses the room
Seeing only him
They have been
Apart too long.

He thinks of their
Intimate times together,
Days of trust,
Complete understanding.

She sits in his lap
Her soft body
Warming his.
Life is complete.

Aauugh! Her breath
Is terrible,
He must change
Her dog food.

Desire

Clowning in the bushes,
the squirrels are full
of themselves.

I stop weeding, approach
the feeding ground tossing
sunflower seeds.

Every morning, same willingness.
I throw open windows, whistle
while hummingbirds

zigzag in the green palace
of hickory and pine.
Mourning doves, full-

bellied, strut in gratitude.
Herons fill the cove:
blue arcs soaring.

How did I come to this?
I reach down, cup
a butterfly. Gold-

lit, my heart, her stillness
electric. Living like a wild-
flower in the errant

design of my garden,
I am newly anointed,
burning with desire.

Carolyn Kreiter-Foronda

(b. 1946, Farmville, Va.) has published four poetry books: *Contrary Visions*, *Gathering Light*, *Death Comes Riding*, and *Greatest Hits*, as well as an anthology of poems, *In a Certain Place*. Her poems, articles, and travel reviews have appeared widely in such publications as *Mid-American Review*, *Prairie Schooner*, *Poet Lore*, *The Montserrat Review*, *Bolivian Times*, *Antietam Review*, and *Passages North*. She has received grants from the Virginia Commission for the Arts and the Council of Basic Education. In 1991 she was named a Virginia Cultural Laureate for her contributions to American Literature.

Carolyn Kreiter-Foronda

The Clearing

The thwack of a backhoe severs
the mint-tinted shoots: those grand
daffodils and irises sprouting.

I flinch as the hollies splinter to earth,
blood-ripe berries scattered around the trunks
of fallen trees. The ground,

rain-moistened, longs for the sheen
of stars, the restful night,
its vigilant moon.

I stoop to gather spring's first lavenders
and golds, the sprigs: rosegray headdresses.
Afraid to tug at stems,

I reach deep into soil to keep
the roots whole. Far from the scarred
clearing, saw-dusted, graceless,

I transplant these bulbs,
nourished by a dove-pair's dance
and the lustrous sun.

In autumn when the land heals,
I'll replant the colors among random holly
growth
and wait for the earth's opulence,

knowing that screech owls
will guard this place
wailing their protective cries.

Carolyn Kreiter-Foronda

Haystacks

A landscape . . . lives . . . by the air and light,
which constantly change.
—Claude Monet, at the opening exhibit of
the Meule Series paintings, May 1891

What is it about ever-changing light,
elusive as it falls on bundled grain,
altering the way we perceive the sight?

Stacks, snow-laced: the blue, marbleized night
hovers above a sun-dappled terrain.
What is it about ever-changing light

that commits us to wonder, yes, delight
as the hay shimmers in feathery rain,
changing how we perceive the transient sight?

You, who govern this world by your own tight
rules, witness how fleeting shadows sustain
a sunset's fire in ever-changing light,

or how a profusion of pink ignites
two misted stacks: the sheen, like porcelain,
changing again the ephemeral sight.

Evening's rose-gold settles over the bright
straw stalks, their burnt-orange hearts lain
bare by a burst of ever-changing light.
Perceive it, shifting. It is in clear sight.

The Johnson Boys

Big Les Johnson and his brother Mo
hurried down to the fashion show.
Having gambled away every nickel they had,
they needed a job, they wanted it bad.
A designer asked if they could mend a dress.
They looked at each other and grinned
"Mo or Les."

Ron Landa

Before retirement in 2000, Ron Landa worked for twenty-seven years as a historian, first with the U.S. Department of State and subsequently the Office of the Secretary of Defense. Since retirement he has been a part-time consultant/contractor for the Historical Office, Office of the Secretary of Defense. He lives in Williamsburg, Va., and began writing poetry last year as a member of the Williamsburg Poetry Workshop.

Ode to Two Hockey Sticks

(Just for the 'll of It)

That lovely sound, the double ll,
it rolls and trills and feels so swell.
No pell nor mell, no willy-nilly,
always to the point, albeit silly.
Compared to vowels, some say it's shallow;
it's one thing, though, I hold most hallow.

Some foreign tongues just can't speak it.
No guillotine will ever tweak it.
While Italians sing out "o bella mia,"
in Sevilla they don a lace mantilla.
Japan never had a god called Zilla,
And it's velly hard to find a Shanghai villa.

So here I'll dwell, a cautious fellow,
loathe to roam, my belly yellow.
But when it comes to raising 'll,
I'll do it often, if not well.

Political Limericks, 2003

(Thank you, Edward Lear!)

Limericks always help me defuse
Frustrations building up from Bush news;
Nonsense news: Nonsense verse—
Which can become a curse—
And with TWO Bushes—so much the worse!

Bush I, II, two campaigns, two Gulf Wars—
It's been almost like revolving doors!
Taxes? BAD! ("READ MY LIPS. . . .")
Plus Bush gaffes, syntax slips—
With long-time hawks now manning the oars. . . .

Mary Antil Lederman

(b. 1925, Los Angeles, Calif.) A.B. from Syracuse University, 1946; M.Ed., University of Va. 1968, retired in 1981 after 23 years as a foreign language teacher/chair at Albemarle High School in Charlottesville, Va. Her poems have appeared in nineteen volumes of *The Poet's Domain*, and the 1993 and the 2003 80th Anniversary Anthologies of the Poetry Society of Virginia. Poetry contest awards include: 1st place, limerick category , 2000 and 2003; and 1st place, 2003, haiku category, in the Poetry Society of Virginia Contest.

Friendly Fire

(the cause of 50% of deaths in the Iraq wars, 1991, 2003).

Daily war "kills" come over the wire
From the smoldering Mid-Eastern pyre,
Parents are not consoled,
Euphemistically told,
Dead sons were victims of "friendly fire."

Mary Antil Lederman

Bush Budget Flip-Flops, 1990:

Who got a fish hook caught in his ear,
And his foot in his lip the same year?
(With a tax about-face
That he tries to debase
As a partisan electioneer.)

With dog Millie again in typeface—
Her bestseller displayed everyplace—
It's too bad her master
Is courting disaster
Between Iraq and fiscal hard place!

Who called Reaganomics pure "voodoo,"
Referring often to "deep doo-doo?"
Who has added his hips
To be watched with lip flips
But cannot say: "No-no, Sununu?"

Like green broccoli is needed for health,
Greenbacks nourish the commonwealth—
And whose grass is greener
For I.R.S. gleaner
Than taxpayers possessing most wealth?

Who is trying loudly to deplore—
At the same time to take credit for—
The budget compromise
That his staff helped devise?
("Barf! Barf! Barf!" Millie says from the floor.)

Handwriting on the Wall, 1990

quote originating in ancient Babylon which is present-day Iraq

Where Edenal civilization
And Abraham's tribal migration
Were thought to have begun
May now become undone
In a world-wide incineration.

The G.O.P. Is Pro-Life, Right? Wrong!

In Florida, justice was thwarted—
And G.O.P. tenets distorted—
When "a know-nothing guy"
Beat a "know-it-all." Why?
The pregnant chads all were aborted!

I'll Be Home for Christmas . . .

Old men start wars young men must die in."
Said a wise old Army veteran. . . .
Home return parents dread:
Body bags in child's stead—
Flag-draped coffins dead heroes lie in.

Mary Antil Lederman

The New Hampshire Primary, February 1992

Cardial Infractions?

(In the news: allegations of a past Jennifer Flowers/Clinton affair.)

Tis the month of red Valentine hearts,
Gooey chocolates and velvety tarts.
When our yens we assuage
And our brains disengage
While we hide all cholesterol charts!

Bimbo news, too, the country devours—
While more substantive scrutiny sours—
But this Valentine's Day
It's a sure bet to say:
"Bill's not sending Gennifer flowers!"

Broccoli Bulimia? Belching Buchanan?

(In the news: Bush hates broccoli;
Bush throws up at formal dinner;
Pat Buchanan moves up in polls.)

With New Hampshire news so abysmal,
And Buchanan making life dismal,
The First Lady's cautious
George doesn't get nauseous—
She's stocked up on more Pepto-Bismol™!

How Trite, How Silly

Easy, it's so easy to ridicule.
"How trite," "How unsophisticated,"
"Not another one of those."

How silly to have that cold weather dullness
Suddenly lift, to have a feeling
Of impending pleasure.

All it needed was a clump of daffodils,
How trite, how silly,
How wonderful they are.

Dagmar Lending

(b. 1932, Long Branch, N.J.) for many years taught children with learning disabilities in Fairfax County, Virginia, where she still lives. Since retiring she has explored teaching classes in genealogy, volunteered in the community, and taken classes, one of which was a poetry workshop at George Mason University. With the encouragement found there, her work has appeared many times in *The Poet's Domain*. She is a member of Pen Women and the Virginia Poetry Society.

Elegance Found

Single white daffodil
in a bud vase
on a polished table

Last of a glorious bunch
mixed bright yellow,
cream and white
turbulently reaching out and up
in all directions
until they faded, drooping

This last has escaped
that burly past
to find sheer elegance alone
in a lead crystal vase

Romantics

Lord Byron's in a fuss
And Shelley's in a swoon,
Wordsworth wanders through the clouds
Looking for the moon.

Keats writes of a vase
And a girl without merci;
Coleridge dreams of Kubla Khan
And drear Philosophy.

They all live together now
In a castle by the sea,
Reciting the poems that brought them Fame
And Immortality!

Joseph Lewis

(b. 1948, Pittsburgh, Pa.) has been published in several previous volumes of *The Poet's Domain*. He lives in Williamsburg, Va.

Bird Watching

I saw my first woodpecker today,
pecking away at a big oak tree,
looking for an insect delicacy.
Such concentration can only be
a product of evolution,
elegant beak and scarlet head
from a million generations.
It flew away to a further tree,
the trunk of the oak was scored,
I wonder if it heard me
when I finally opened the door
to let sunlight fall on the floor.
Or whether it knew that I
wanted to join it in the sky.
But in the scheme of things
words must do over wings.

Nancy Lexo

was born in Mt. Vernon, N.Y. and now lives in Mt. Vernon, Va. She is an elementary school teacher in Fairfax County, Va., and lives with her wonderful husband and three daughters. She loves to write children's poetry and short stories and has had several of them published in the past.

Marcus McAnder McKnee

I want to see some other place,
I want to fill some other space,
Said Marcus McAnder McKnee.
He took his shoes with feet inside,
And walked until he found a ride,
To places he would rather be.

I'd like to live by mountains rising to the sky,
So off he went in search of such perfection to
the eye.
He found those hills aglitter, shining in the sun,
And shrugged his shoulders dolefully now his
quest was won.

Maybe it's the sea I want, the smell of sweet
salt air,
And off he went two thousand miles to fill his
latest care.
The waves lapped at the feet of Marcus
McAnder McKnee,
And added one more notch in his latest travel
spree.

It's the city I want, the roar of the crowd,
The hustle and bustle, the traffic, the music
blaring loud.
Give me the sights and sounds of a million
people plus,
Marcus McAnder McKnee caught the very
next Greyhound bus.

Nancy Lexo

I want to feel all stressed out, I want to smell
the smog,
I want to always hurry up, my life will be a fog.
Could this be the end of my search, he asked
himself one day?
There's got to be some other where, I need to
get away.

The desert, that's it, I need the hot dry air,
I'll leave the city behind and move myself out
there.
With nothing in sight but sand, he stood and
looked around,
And Marcus McAnder McKnee knew it was
home that he was bound.

I've seen the golden mountains, I've seen the
deepest sea,
I've seen every place on Earth, said Marcus
McAnder McKnee.
Of all the places I have been, I liked the first
one best,
I think I'll start my journey home and give my
feet a rest.

Nancy Lexo

From Here to There

Along the road from here to there,
Are swerves and curves to take with care.
Although at times we move too fast,
And miss the sights that make our past.

Somewhere between here and there you might
just lose your way,
And if you do, rest your sights before they run
astray.
Keep both feet moving down the path that
surely ends up there,
Don't worry if you trip or fall, you'll learn to
move with care.

If at times you're not sure why you're moving
down the road,
Stop awhile and rest that soul that ever bears
the load.
Squeeze your mind of troubles, leave them by
the side,
And kick away the pieces that seem to break
your stride.

The journey's full of pitfalls, ruts and potholes too,
And as you move around them you find life's
biggest clue.
With each and every step, you're closer to
your goal,
Of taking what was incomplete and making it
a whole.

Triolet

A poem can fall apart
while one struggles with a rhyme.
We hope to make a work of art.
But a poem can fall apart
while we wonder how to start
or delay it for another time.
A poem can fall apart
While one struggles with a rhyme.

Jean Leyman

(b. 1927, Seattle, Wash.) has lived most of her life in the Washington, D.C. area, with some years in Hawaii, the Philippines, and Okinawa. She studied poetry at the University of Washington with Lawrence Zillman and more recently with Michael Fitzgerald in Winchester, Va. She belongs to the National League of American Pen Women and is director of the St. Elmo's Poetry Readings. Among recent publications are the *American Tanka*, *Potpourri*, the *Lyric*, and *Chesapeake*.

Twisted

No longer what you once were
among the twisted metal
          the broken glass;
together, as one, bleeding and
trapped with a death that once
represented life.

Now, like your auto,
far beyond recognition:
falling asleep at the wheel was
your last act;
          your mortal life has
lost all its meaning.

Chain saws, pry tools
firefighters cutting away the wreckage.
You'll never know the image
painted on another's mind:
that other meaning
for the word, twisted.

D. S. Lliteras

(b.1949, New York, N.Y.) has a master of fine arts degree from Florida State University. He is the author of eight books, which have received national and international acclaim. In the last eighteen years, his poetry and short stories have appeared in numerous periodicals and anthologies. His most recent novel, *Jerusalem's Rain*, was released in July, 2003. He is a retired professional firefighter and lives in Virginia Beach, Va. with his wife, Kathleen.

D. S. Lliteras

Destruction

Askewed watercolors
smudged and cracked and
nameless with damage;
hanging in a hallway
in a burned out structure;
from the blaze a kind of death
face to face on both walls:
landscapes and seascapes
unnoticed losses by firefighters
    ankle deep in water,
    soot-covered and tired
    from the battle
overlooked decor by employees
    their existence forgotten,
    astonished and exhausted
    by the spectacle of destruction.

Upon one thing
my loneliness is amplified,
my sadness is focused
upon its broken beauty,
upon its last surviving moment
briefly captured by my hushed silence,
my admiration, my appreciation,
while standing before the remains of
a "still life."

D. S. Lliteras

Friday Night

Haphazard
people and vehicles parked
and dressed in red and blue
flashing lights.

At the center:
an ambulance, housing
a gunshot victim
surrounded by paramedics,
firefighters, the police, and

a hopeless mob
living at the end of the line
and called the social services of
low cost housing.

The Puzzler

A crossword puzzle junky, I,
I do one every day.
So weird words always occupy
my jumbled repartée.

Some words are tough to use, although
I leap at every chance;
like **galop** is, of course you know,
a nineteenth-century dance.

Ennead is a group of nine;
an emmet is an ant.
A pair of cows is called a **kine**,
and jargon is a **cant**.

The usefulness you may refute
but first let me submit:
an **ugli** is Jamaican fruit;
a voucher is a **chit**.

Weird words when used make you seem sage,
as wise as you can be.
Like **verso** is the left hand page,
and **erst** is formerly.

A llama is—I bet you know—
but if you're not too sure:
domesticated **guanaco**;
now isn't that obscure?

The spawn of oysters is a **spat**,
while **agar** is a gel.
Include these morsels in your chat;
they have the sweetest smell.

Edward Lull

(b.1932, North Wales, Pa.) began his professional career as a naval officer where he served primarily in submarines. Mr. Lull began writing poetry at age 65. In 1998 he joined The Poetry Society of Virginia, and he currently serves as its president. He has published poems in several anthologies, including earlier issues of *Poet's Forum*. This year, Mr. Lull published his first book, a historical novel written in blank verse, entitled *Cabin Boy to Captain: a Sea Story.*

And so, dear friends, do not pass by
those puzzles with crossed words.
Your word bank they will magnify;
you'll join my class of nerds!

Called to Serve

It wasn't called a war, but he was called to serve.
Just months ago they swayed to big band sounds
and promised to share their lives;
but now she saw him off—a soldier far too soon.

He loved her and he loved the land;
he'd serve his time, then back to Georgia's soil.
He knew that General Doug would keep his word:
win the war and send the boys back home.

To infantry he went—a grunt—as he was called.
His training—very brief—a ship then took him west.
Korea's ice and snow were half a world away
from Georgia's warming sun.

Realities of war were closing on him fast;
his peaceful world would change this bitter day.
His company called to spearhead an attack,
the sickness in his gut confirmed his fear.

Are those we face just farmers much like me,
called to fight for reasons we don't know?
Should I take lives because I'm told I must;
Can I expect God's mercy if I kill?

His squad on point, they squirmed
through bloody snow—he hardly felt the cold.
Grenades and mortars boomed ahead,
while bullets zinged off rocks and icy banks.

Edward Lull

Across a ridge he came face-to-face
with a young Oriental man in drab gray uniform,
lying on his side, eyes wide in lifeless stare,
gaping hole in his forehead.

Startled and sickened by the sudden encounter
he arose from a pool of his own vomit.
At that vulnerable instant he felt the searing pain;
his thigh was hit with force that threw him down.

He did his best to slow the oozing blood.
MEDIC! MEDIC! He knew he needed help;
the others on the ground were still and cold;
the battle had moved on; he felt alone.

He called again, but felt his voice grow weak;
perhaps some rest would help restore his
sapping strength.
His pain had eased, the snow a restful bed;
he said his evening prayers—and drifted off.

****

They sent his casket home; no bands nor
fanfare there;
no gold star to display; no closure for the pain.
While politicians postured, he gave his country all;
his parents and his sweetheart mourned alone.

He sleeps beneath his Georgia clay—unsung.
It wasn't called a war—but he was called to die.

The Foreign Correspondent Daydreams on the VRE*

The battle began in heaven.
All day the war clouds darkly rose,
Smoking out the light of the world.

Listen to the rainstorm's speech:
Healing, heavy droplets, single splashes,
Raindrop words arouse rainforests.

The humid air balloons, builds up
A bomb detonating rolling thunder;
Lightning muzzle-flashes, opens fire.

Commuter rails shuttle us
Between war zones in the mind.
Telephone poles blur by the glass.

Monsoon flashbacks, jungle downpours,
Earth tremors and the heavenly wails—
Sounds like martyrdom in the Holy Land.

Summer storm echoes old warfare.
Our memory relives explosions:
Mortars, "fire in the hole,"

Incoming, sappers in the sewers.
Saigon once sounded like Jerusalem.
No blessings rain on holy wars.

New threats follow the fuse and flash.
No peace seeks the space, the silence
After the storm, just more flooding.

Michael Hugh Lythgoe

(b. Evansville, Ind.) retired as an air force officer. He was selected as a contributor to *Invitation to Poetry*, forthcoming in 2004 (W.W. Norton), the latest "Favorite Poem Project," edited by Robert Pinsky, Poet Laureate of the United States, 1997–2000. His poems have appeared in volumes 4 through 20 of *The Poet's Domain*.

*Virginia Railway Express commuter service runs from Broad Run, Virginia to Washington, D C

Michael Hugh Lythgoe

The 7:27 leaves Manassas
Like Lee's retreat from Richmond.
Look for revenge; live for the end.

Ugly shrouds of fog wrap the tracks.
The clatters pass over triple canopy,
Hiding creeks, switchbacks—cross

A border, a boundary, a frontier.
Relive a Cold War, not romance
Aboard the Orient Express.

A bold sun burns up the mist
Like secrets. Wild yellow flowers
Grapple, eyeing tattoos on trellis legs:

The tribal art of DC's urban guerrillas.
Imagine nearing Berlin, the Gestapo
and SS are loading boxcars. Aircraft

Strafe targets as the train crosses
The bridge into a scarred city.
See the hopelessness along tracks.

Graffiti murals and war-torn ruins
Kidnap victims in Chechnya.
Daydreaming can be dangerous.

The conductor calls our destination.
We exit our imagination,
Arriving at Union station.

Michael Hugh Lythgoe

Chanticleer in the Caribbean

La Senora Ojea
Remembers Chanticleer's
Morning songs
In Sabana, Puerto Rico.
She loved the crowing
As much as rhythmic
Slow rains on tin roofs
And open shutters, delicious
Swings in the hammock
Under the thatch shelter
At her grandfather's,
A land of green breezes.
He took her on the ferry ride
From Catano shanty town
Over to San Juan for *queso*
Derretido at La Bombonera.
Now the Bacardi distillery
Lures tourists there
With citrus-flavored rums.
Always afraid of birds,
Even their feathers,
She never neared the rooster
Who sang for her,
Knew only the silent "vane"
Turning in the wind for her,
The invisible singer
On her island of childhood.
Later she saw the bantam
And his harem foraging
Around ramshackle Virginia
          Until
Now, returning to her island.

Michael Hugh Lythgoe

Chanticleer

Is still there, screwing
Around in Guaynabo, a singer,
A contrary protector
Of the hen house of his past,
Parading his cock's comb.
He calls out to her before daylight
And later—as she is leaving—
Chanticleer sings out
At the San Juan airport,
Crowing from a pet carrier—
A traveler, too,
Carted off someplace to fight
Illegally—maybe Maryland or Miami—
Aspiring to resume vocalizing
If he does not die entertaining.

5/26/03—Memorial Day

Weather wise today is dull and dreary—
A gloomy day, but in my eyes it's okay
Because gloominess matches sadness,
And a shroud of sadness well-fits this
special Memorial Day.

Once each year the day is set aside for
Public ceremony and private meditation
To memorialize and remember sons and
Daughters, brothers and sisters, dear
Friends, and all cherished others who
While in our military services perished in
wars that have past.

I deem today's national holiday as
Special, for now we have a new crop
Of war-time deaths—those who fell
Just yesterday; and the crop of fresh-killed
Is still growing with deaths happening on
This very day of memorial observations in
A war that is yet not over, and its end we
know not when.

So deaths, we know, there will be more
On that killing field where humankind
Began—the spot of earth that was Paradise,
The Eden of short duration made so by His
Intervention because of manifested weaknesses
By the Garden's human population.

Seymour Z. Mann

(b. 1921, Chicago, Ill.) from Alexandria, Va. is professor emeritus, CUNY where he served on the faculties of Hunter College, John Jay College, and as a member of the University's doctoral faculty in political science. His poetic efforts were included in seven previous volumes of *The Poet's Domain*, and he is honored to have his poems in the company of fellow poets and friends whose work also appears in the pages of this volume.

Seymour Z. Mann

Those who have fallen in the recent weeks,
Those who fell today and those who'll
Fall tomorrow will move easily into the
Memories of those who mourn the lost ones
Because this is a Memorial Day for the
Freshly-killed whose souls are just wending
Their ways on the journey from planet earth
To their heavenly destinations.

There is sad irony in the place of the fresh deaths
Memorialized today, with the memorial ceremonies
And private remembrances all cloaked in a veil of
Ambivalence about this war's purpose and what
The nature of its end game and fall-out will be; all
Has engendered sadness on this day of leaden skies.
It is gloominess to match the sadness.

At the Gallery

I said, in answer to her question so deftly asked,
It's exceptionally beautiful and exceedingly
subtle in color.
Said she, *You're so discerning, and the sensitivity*
of your observation sets me to yearning.
I said, *As it does for me. I'd hang it on the wall*
just above my bed.
Said she, *for me it should hang where my opening*
eyes would see it in the morning.
I said, *Especially I like it because it truly tells*
so clear a story.
Said she, *Oh, I thought the same, and the figures, though*
quite abstract, convey strength and glory.
I asked then, *Will you buy it?*
She countered fast, *Would you?*
I answered last, *Of course, I would*—I lied.

Seymour Z. Mann

Senseless Sensitivities

Bitter in her mouth was the taste of her
utter failure.
She was greatly wounded by the rejection
so sudden and severe.
The words of he who had so unexpectedly,
and abruptly exited
reverberated with ferocious noise on the
walls of her skull.

They burned in her brain, and dug deeply
into the bowel of her being.
The room now seethed with sharp acridity
as if it were choked with smoke
from his many fire-like departing words.
Her senses were at the edge of
aching rawness so that she was sickened
from the odor of her own perfume.
And the once tantalizing enthrall of the
pheromones that still lingered,
were now only the soul-shaking reminders
of how sorely she was wounded.

First Blood

The father stood before me beaming.
His son of ten years—
Pee-Wee football player,
T-ball player,
Junior soccer player.
He had shown me all the pictures,
And today he had another.

The father, so proud of this only child
After so many barren years,
There would be no more after him
As there were none before
For this man and his wife;
Too risky after so many miscarriages.

He handed me the photo
Saying just two words,
"His first."

Lifeless graying trees in the background
Awaiting the first blanketing snowfall.
There, centered in the five by seven,
The boy was kneeling,
Dressed in camouflaged overalls
And, like his father standing before me,
Grinning broadly,
Showing off his imperfect teeth.

A small doe with that too-familiar
Thousand-yard stare
Lying in the photo's foreground.

John G. Marshall

has known that within him were stories to tell in prose and poetry form. A part time student at Thomas Nelson Community College in Hampton, Va., John credits the reawakening of the muse to TNCC's creative writing courses. Encouraged by his professors, fellow students, and his wife of 33 years, John is now attempting to get some of his work in print. Outside of TNCC's annual writing contest, this is his first success.

John G. Marshall

Her small but bare swollen teats
showing signs of recent activity
from a late-born nursing fawn,
As crimson lips gave evidence
Of her demise.

The boy grasped her small ears,
Held up her lifeless head,
And I wondered,
Were they still warm
In his small tender hands,
And would he cut one off
And wear it around his neck as a trophy
On a string.

Looking sadly at the picture,
At the child who had tasted
His first blood,
My heart was heavy
For the youngster
Who had been taught to see
Not a life
But a living target.

John G. Marshall

The Sleepwalker

We used to walk hand in hand
Barefoot through grassy fields,
And made love under the willow trees.
You were so beautiful then,
And in my dreams we haven't changed
From those days past.

I wake more slowly now
Not wanting to let go
Of those scenes of you and us;

Images of the way things were
Before I went away to that foreign land.
Reality is quite different
Because I am not the man I was then.
What's not been crippled by mine
Has been destroyed by mind.

You tried but couldn't live with what I have become.
My misdirected rage has severed our love.
Now I have nothing but these four walls,
A nurse named Betty (how ironic),
And my dreams of walking barefoot
Among the willows
In search of you.

Today Betty chastises,
"What's on your feet?"
As she observes my newly gangrenous digits.

"Grass stain,
I walk in my sleep,"
I reply contemptuously,
As in my chariot she places me
And my lifeless legs.

Felicia Mason

is a novelist and poet who lives in Virginia. Her most recent novels include *Testimony and Sweet Accord*. Her poetry has been published in periodicals; *The Journal of Ethnic Studies*, and *The Poet's Domain*, volume 18. Novels exploring the themes of transformation and redemption will be published in 2004, including *Sweet Harmony* in January and *Sweet Devotion* in February.

Street-Corner Blues

Brothers on the street corner
looking around
can't be productive
no jobs abound.
Smoking that weed
toking that crack
lifting a bottle
in a brown paper sack.

Sista walks by
swinging her hips
she's got a purpose . . .
turn another trick.
Didn't want no babies
but still got three
waitin' on her man
and a judge's decree.

Cops drift by
showing a threat
but ain't nothing happenin'
'cept a coupla bets.
Money changes hands
and the deals are done
just another day of business
on the stretch called Jefferson.

Dance

Brown girl warm
skin so smooth
looking like shelter
feeling her groove.

Brown boy smiles
loving her sway
waiting for the welcome
to her honey-kissed way.

Felicia Mason

The Poet Speaks of Truth

This form leaves little room
for shadows so easily concealed
in long works of fractured conflict.
In four hundred pages of prose
the truth is there—where no one can see it.
But the poet has no place
to shelter the knowing
or to shield the significant
and so it sits on the page
waiting to be embraced.

Altered Perception Suite

Mental Image

Much like a gazelle
I fly—spirit racing by
smooth, quick, filled with grace.

Reality

Lumbering footsteps
heavy along the floorboards
tired, aching, sigh.

Class: Acts of the Apostles

Dear Dr. Franklin:

It was good of you to love us,
two angry orphaned girls
who sat and railed
blindly blasphemed and flailed
questioning every doctrine.
Seminarians squirmed appalled
but you appeared enthralled
with us strongly struggling there.

Like moths under a pin we were—
so rapt and out of breath
so close to death
nailed so firmly to our cross.

Mary Burton Haskell McKenzie

(b.1926, Baltimore, Md.) grew up in Richmond where her ancestors lived in pre-Revolutionary days. She began to write and contribute poems to periodicals while in grade school at Westhampton. In high school at St. Catherine's she studied with Margaret McGing. Currently she lives in Atlanta with her husband, Kermit, and cats, Mia, Max, and Marcus Aurelius.

Eclipse: Nash Middle School

Children crouch huddled
in the lunchroom
blinds drawn
the sky invisible.
Others cower in the hall
watching TV
under the watchful eyes
of teachers.

While in the inner court
rebellious faculty
steal furtive glances
at the forbidden sun
awesome and searing,
risking Icarian doom
for one, brief, transcendent
Ecstasy.

Mary Burton Haskell McKenzie

Yearly Pilgrimage Home

Uncle Asbury,
actively engaged in the process
of dying,
quietly watches TV
not talking much
a little about what hurts
what ails this body
he's now abandoning.

I am dismayed!
Only last year, planting
absorbed him.
Head wagged, jowls swung,
eyes twinkled roguishly
as he described
the nutty neighbor woman
who shot at him
in his orchard.
Now no fruits are tended
and no one shoots.
Great grandchildren flow
swiftly around him
like a river leaving behind
an island filled
with ruins.

Awkwardly I search for him
reach back into our yesterdays
and onward toward
our mutual deaths,
stumbling with sad words,
trying somehow, desperately
to say good-bye
with love.

Mary Burton Haskell McKenzie

A Dead Soldier to His Child

Dear, do not dream
I love you less because
I vanished
as you clung
to me the most.

I will return to you,
a penitent ghost,
if I can bend away
the sensate bars
which mar perceiving me.

Forgive me finally
for all your days of yearning
spent in vain,
all of the bitter,
hopeless, endless pain

which I have willed you,
bequeathed helplessly.
For I have watched you there
lost and forlorn
blaming yourself

for loss I left behind,
searching the darkest caverns
of your mind,
viewing the awesome day
when you were born.

And still I would protect you
if I might
from hideous demons
gibbering in the night.

Mary Burton Haskell McKenzie

Winter Driving

Angora gray clouds hover
enfolding a frozen earth
clenched in cold misery,
dull straw and faded blues . . .

Yet green, too!
Always the evergreens
singing, singing
of birth, of eternity!

And we
reaching for meaning
in our barren state
stretch up
like the cold bare trees
black against a bright sky,
like lace,
and feel the touch of God,
like sun
also upon our face.

Lucky Us

Lucky for babies they're so cute,
else how could these self-centered mites,
these greedy, sticky yammerers,
these snot-nosed yukkers-up survive?

Lucky their parents see no flaws,
dote on their yawns in miniature,
their tiny hands and pink toesies,
and proudly tend their diaper wastes.

Lucky these parents stay enthralled
when dark hormonal chemistry
transforms their babes before their eyes
to wild rebellious teenagers.

And then that same weird alchemy
turns them to grown-up aliens
that somehow parents still hold dear.
Lucky any of us are here.

Time's Penmanship

I like to watch my sleeping love,
how rest smoothes wrinkles from her face,
restores the beauty I once knew,
when we were young and love was new.

I like to see her wake again,
watch time deftly re-etch her face,
with beauty of a richer kind,
our years of love in every line.

Frank N. Megargee

(b. 1917, Philadelphia, Pa.) is a retired newspaperman now free to write what comes to mind, This is his ninth appearance in *The Poet's Domain*.

Frank N. Megargee

The Veil

Out for a morning stroll I found
the chain-link fence I always pass,
laced with dew-beaded spider webs,
its wired diamonds opaque with them,
so that it seemed a tapestry,
suspended there all silvery.

Then suddenly a stray sunbeam
pierced the early morning mist
and turned the fence to jeweled veil,
shimmering with rainbow hues,
a work of art, gift of the sun,
shown to an audience of one.

Too soon the mist closed in again,
returning fence to grey fabric.
I waited for another beam,
but when one finally filtered through
I guess the angle wasn't right,
the vision never came to light.

But I felt blest as I strolled on
by that brief glimpse into what seemed
a transcendental realm that lies
just beyond our mortal eyes.

Frank N. Megargee

Yard Work

Sweat-band darkening on his brow,
my neighbor on the hottest days,
strides behind his old push mower,
spurning power's noise and fumes,
clickety-clacking summer's song,
as back and forth he shaves his lawn.

"I like to mow," he once told me,
"gripping the handles, feet on the ground,
putting some oomph in what I do.
Miss that at the office, you know,
a lot of oomph builds up in me,
and mowing helps to set it free."

As if that didn't say it all,
he thought aloud, "Besides, out here
I get to smell the new cut grass,
glance up at the sky now and then,
make sure that all is well up there,
and feel how small I am down here."

He beams at me through gleaming sweat,
and I think how desperately
we seek some solace in our lives,
some assurance we have a place
in our magnificent surround,
and in what odd ways it's found.

Chinese Restaurant

to Meihua

red booth, smooth
dark-glossed quiet womb,
translucent amber foaming
in frosted glass,
lemon slice in ice water,
tipped clicking rims,
white cloth napkins, chopsticks
laid in folded paper,
red tasseled lantern, gold dragon
boldspread along wall,
black-striped yellow angelfish
angling languid, coral reef
flower-animals waving slow
in lighted water, bean curd
brown thick sauce spicy,
rice sloped hot
in fragrant bowls,
squat round-lipped cups
of dark tea steaming,
sweet oranges, tan shells crisp
yielding paper fortunes,
laughing
over clink of coins bright
on cool glass,
slip out laughing
into night
heavy
under hot moon

Merrill Miner

is the pen name of Nancy Merrill Miner Canning. Born and raised in Philadelphia, Pa., Ms. Miner received a B.A. in oriental studies from Barnard College, Columbia University, and an M.A. in east asian studies from Stanford University. Ms. Miner has taught English in Japan and China as well as in Williamsburg, Va. She recently initiated Poets' Forum, held monthly under the auspices of the Williamsburg Regional Library.

Merrill Miner

Mama E

Mama E, when autumn comes
I think of you—fall days'
crisp crinkled leaves, slow-falling leaf-drift
curlicues in morning mist, gold dew-hushed
stillness, oakleaf crunch in leafy woods,
squirrel silverwhisk round and round
rough treetrunks, acorn wreathcrowns ground-
spilled,
split pods, slim husks reckless strewn
in dry grass, starlings' chitter in tangled vines,
crowcall raucous deepwood echo, wing-slow
pulselift skyward,
blackwinged distant scattered sweep
across crystal skies. I see
your quickbrown eyes and crispcurled hair,
your earthen bowl heaped high with walnuts,
autumn leaves on your small table
bright under glass. I see
the woven scarf you loved
of orange-red draped waiting
on the hall chair by the door.

April Frost

Lovely tree outside my window,
You blossom through one hot March night.
Now sub-freezing breezes threaten
to take away your blossoms bright.
Dad says he would rather
Have his Winter come ere Spring;
Instead April frosts threaten
to put an end to everything.

Jacqueline S. Moore

This is the last poem written by Jacqueline S. Moore, a frequent contributor to *The Poet's Domain*. She wrote it while in a nursing home during her last illness. She died at home April 11, 2002. It is submitted with permission of her husband, James R. Moore.

Evolution

Deep inside
It all goes deep.
That's what brings you back again and again.
Cause that's what we do—
We irritate and gyrate right inside the brain,
We go to the heart and wake in the deep dark
hours where we leave you thinking how
You hate cause you can't figure out what it is
we're talkin' bout.
So we take you out and try to make you see
what was there again and again.
And you might not like what you read but you
ride the train.
That's right!
You take the lousy trip and smile.

Lu Motley

semi-retired, was an adjunct professor of English composition at J. Sargeant Reynolds Community College for twelve years. She is currently creating a writing program for students in the Richmond schools after a stimulating six week summer session teaching a class she designed called "Ghostbusters," mostly about Edgar Allen Poe; and a playwriting class based on Shakespeare's *Midsummer Night's Dream* in which six promising playwrights wrote and produced six original plays.

Obit

for Carl Motley

I read his obit this morn as my heart ached for
things unsaid.
I was there as the "mother of his boys."
Sounded like I was his mistress. Oh well . . .
Still, there were no words which told of all the
years which came together,
Or the last days as he suffered dreadfully
while we three who had once
been his family prayed and rubbed his
taut, contracted with pain, stomach,
praying for the death monster to leave
and let us be as we were before.
"He was a passionate gardener and artist."

Lu Motley

I would add, "All of the above," then, I would
add the word "lover" to that list.
My first, the best I've ever had. I recommend
him for heaven's gates and thank God I
knew him thus.
Even his two dogs were in there—"Marcel
and Daucas,"
Now left to miss the walks,
expressions of admiration for
Marcel's beauty.
Years ago we'd had fourteen cats when the
boys were young,
a rare breed with blue eyes and six
toes and all white coats.
Whatever happened to them all?
Obituaries are such limited things—a tiny
piece stuffed into a small space on the back
page of the Metro section about all the
years of living.
It would take the side of a mountain to cover
the details,
Step by step,
performing his music, raising our boys, fighting,
loving, praying, working . . . till after
twenty years, parting, then
learning to live apart.
No words can tell that story.

Who Wants to Listen to the Clock?

My house could be neat with everything in place
But it's not.
There are papers on the floor, crayons on the table
And shoes piled at the door.

Little feet come running through
"Nana, where are you?" they shout.
In the kitchen, on the porch or
somewhere near about.

I wouldn't have it any other way
Tick . . . Tock . . . Tick . . . Tock
Who wants to listen to the clock?
Neat and clean can be awfully lonely.

I'd rather have Kool-Aid™, Gatorade™, or
lemonade running down the counter
Sand on the floor, cookies baking in the oven,
Water running in the tub, or
Voices scrapping over who walks the dog.

I actually like bandages,
Mercurochrome™, and
chocolate covered Oreo™ lips!

I love questions like:
What do you have to eat?
What can we make? or
Can I spend the night?

"Let's go out on the boat.
I want to go fishing!" my grandson shouts.
Shove the boat away from the dock!
Who wants to listen to the clock?

Peggy Newcomb

has a B.S. in chemistry from Mary Washington College of the University of Virginia. She is a chemistry teacher in York High School, Yorktown Va. In 1997, she won first place, non-fiction, in the Chesapeake Bay Writers Conference Contest.

Rider

The butterfly rests on the umbilical cord
of the pool sweeper as it moves
quietly through the water

The cord dips under the surface, reappears
The butterfly, intact, flutters its wings
and continues its silent ride

Stone Statue

Mysterious monk
Face half concealed by his cowl
Striding swiftly
Destination unknown

Barbara L. Nuñes

(b. 1937, Cleveland, Oh.) lives in Northern Virginia and is a member of the National League of American Pen Women. She is also a member of the Fairfax Area League of Women Voters and the Potomac Branch of the American Begonia Society. She loves to play her mountain dulcimer and create watercolor paintings.

Crowtalk

Crows came to live in the trees
of my maturity. Their voices said that I was
home and all was well. I wondered that
this raucous crew gave me such peace.

From birth to fifteen months I was
sole owner of my mom and dad,
a lavishment of devotion carried
in my belly all my life.

Those same summers of my infancy
were bathed in the conversation of
crows calling in the treetops.
My family left that home when I was three.

As a man I am warmed by memory
linking the sound of crows to my
mother's and my father's love;
Crowtalk is the song of happiness.

Robert Parke, Jr.

Robert Parke, Jr., demographer, was born in Buffalo N.Y., and was a 36-year resident of Alexandria Va. He died at home on November 5, 1998. He held an A.B. and an M.A. in sociology and taught undergraduate sociology at Brown University and Muhlenberg College. He moved to Washington, DC in 1959 where he subsequently made significant contributions in behalf of the American public. He was a deacon and past moderator of Little River United Church of Christ in Annandale, led adult church school classes, and wrote religious songs. At his death, he was writing poetry.

Robert Parke, Jr.

Hearing Loss

The murmur of her lovely voice gets through
but these days I am hearing less and less
of what she says. And so I guess—
I tell her what I think I heard and
what I'm going to do.

After dinner she says to me (I guess)
thank you for doing the carving.
I say I was glad to do the carving.
She smiles and says that what she asked
was for me to take out the garbage.

She speaks to me about our wills
and (guessing) I dissent, asking
why she wants the wills to speak of diapers.
She smiles and says she said,
"If I should die first."

Should I demand that she repeat herself
or warn her to speak up?
This way's more fun.
I tell her what I thought I heard
and answer cheerfully. It works.
It gets the garbage out.

Robert Parke, Jr.

Side Effects

My cancer is an abstraction.
Real is fatigue that sends me home
from work before my work is done.
Real is being stuck with needles,
pushing an IV pole with a wheel missing,
losing clumps of hair in the shower,
puking in the parking lot.

These angel visitors alert me
with all my faculties intact
to live the balance of my life
in the awareness of my coming death.
My life is not chopped off by a heart attack,
my speech is not disabled by a stroke,
Alzheimer's does not melt my brain.

Warned, and given this sweet time,
I write, I grieve my father, enjoy my daughters.
Making fatigue my friend, I take naps, reduce
work.
I cherish the web I live in with my wife.
We sit together talking as the twilight comes.

Two Routes to China

When I was a child, I dug a hole toward China,
but four feet into the loamy soil, I found no
mud-covered pagodas,
heard no silk swishing through the Peking air.
Earthworms were digging tunnels
through the walls of clay I had just made
as if seeking routes to China too under the grass.
Instead of envisioning the Forbidden City
through veils of dust
and the Great Wall snaking underground,
I merely struck random rocks with my small shovel
and gave up on the attempt.

In China it is said that the mulberry
sacrifices itself to the woodsman's ax as paper,
its trunk disemboweled of bark for sheets
where Chinese poets plant their visions
with characters that sprawl across the page like
dark, twisted twigs.
When I was twelve, I sat under the trees in
California
in a strip of park above the ocean, leafing
through Dante,
blown about like a broken branch in a hellish
hurricane
beside the disembodied spirits of Paolo and
Francesca,
climbed the rungs of a purgatorial mountain,
and swirled with angels in celestial pinwheels
of light.
On forests of mulberry Tu Fu, Wang Wei, and
Li Po
sowed other visions, spreading like seed all
over the world.

David J. Partie

(b. 1944, Detroit, Mich.) lives in Lynchburg, Va. and teaches English and Spanish at Liberty University. He earned his Ph.D. in comparative literature from the University of Southern California. He won the Karma Deane Ogden Prize in 1991, the Brodie Herndon Prize in 1997, and the Carleton Drewy Prize in 2000 from the Poetry Society of Virginia. His poems have appeared in several volumes of *The Poet's Domain* and in the 1993 and 2003 anthologies of the Poetry Society of Virginia. He has been listed three times in *Who's Who Among America's Teachers* and will be included in the 2004 edition of *Who's Who inAmerica*.

David J. Partie

In my study tonight, reading by lamplight,
watching snow descend upon the lawn
lettered with tracks of deer and dog,
I know now I could have saved that child a lot
of trouble.
To find my way to Shanghai, to the palaces of
jade, or to the stars,
all I had to do was climb a tree.

A Tale for Mother Goose

MiRan Powell

(b.1964, Plainview, Tex.), professional actress and editor, member of A.S.I.A., a theatre company dedicated to bringing Asian American stories to the stage. She has been writing poetry for over fifteen years and resides in Sterling, Va. Her poetry also appears in volume 16 of *The Poet's Domain*.

Where has all the energy gone
for chasing Tinkerbell's stars—
spent in waiting for seedlings to sprout,
in lining my nest with twigs
Nothing will stick to these walls of glass
My children's hands slide down my womb
and out, out they go
to play in someone else's yard,
nestle in someone else's breast

I don't care that I am sick,
fragile, and bent at the waist with pain
I don't care that I am growing old
day after day after day
But I see the tree is withering
and wonder why the fruit is bad
why nothing grows here . . .
why it only breaks my heart
one piece at a time and yet defines
singly, unequivocally, each exhalation of breath
until the last, the final.

A child cries in the distance,
and I think, somehow, "it is mine"
A nephew lives in the distance,
and I think, "he should be mine"
All golden sweetness, baby face:
"Nana" "humbry" "Why?"
And the empty space rips through me
from the inside out, leaving jagged edges
that get jostled from time to time

Other than that, I am fine really fine
Because the closeness of the distance

surrounds me like a moat
Invisible, silent, industrial-strength window
from which I peer and smile,
reach with fingertips to touch
See, sometimes in the distance
is as close as one may come
When love can look to reach the stars
but not what lies beyond

September Morn

Here, take my hand
First one step, then two
I'm right beside you
as we fly to Heaven's gate
We are so high
We are so high

MiRan Powell

Birthday

A big fat hen, pink dress, and cake—
that was then when good luck came
from eating embedded eggs
buried deep within a chicken's womb,
and mothers and fathers lived
beyond memory's unfocused lens.

I think the luck ran out in 1948,
and I could not go back
to retrieve family treasure or apologize to ancestors,
because Truman thought two countries
are better than one,
and because America was my destiny.

I don't expect much for birthdays now.
I discovered in the first year of my orphanhood
that mother's love is most sublime
and difficult to imitate.
But once in a while, I have dreams
of a big fat hen, pink dress, and cake.

Frazzled
or
How Elinor Wylie Might Have Rewritten Dorothy Parker's "Resume"

I was, being human, born alone.
I am, being woman, hard beset—
I live by squeezing from a stone
The little nourishment I get.

—Wylie, *Let Now No Charitable Hope*

Now that no charitable hope
Exists, shall I apply my nose
To gas pipe, sniff that Perfect Rose?
Or shall my weight extend a rope?
Perhaps a poison, spite of pain?
A razor's cool and creamy kiss
Across my throat? Or why not this—
A bullet, bursting through my brain?

Ah, me! I simply can't decide
Which of these sweet outrageous masks
Best fits me, as Death's lovely bride. . . .
I know! I just won't "squeeze the stone,"
Refrain from further tiresome tasks,
Die undernourished and alone.

Richard Raymond III

(b. 1930, Cambridge, N.Y.), retired engineer, now living in Roanoke, Va. Former Marine Corps officer; retired from Virginia Army National Guard; author of historical articles to military magazines; winner of numerous poetry prizes in contests by World Order of Narrative and Formalist Poets, The Poetry Society of Virginia, etc. He has been published in thirteen volumes of *The Poet's Domain*.

Sheep

It was easy
When someone else's priest sinned.
I sneered at the folly of Catholic faith
In man:
The white collar coiled 'round his neck
Signifying what?
A snake in his trousers ready to strike
To penetrate
The innocence of childhood,
To rape!
And now that the shoeprint of lust
Dirties the pants
Of my preacher, a man,
Having solicited sex
From a streetwalking decoy
Shatters my sanctuary.
No joy resides in my spirit.

Dorothy Marie Rice

a native of Pittsylvania County, Virginia, is currently the literature and history resource teacher at the Arts and Humanities Center. Mrs. Rice has coauthored three books. Two of the books are about Maggie Lena Walker, the Richmond banker, philanthropist and community activist. *Miss Maggie and Pennies to Dollars* were co-written with her cousin Muriel Miller Branch. The third book: *The Seventeenth Child* was co-written with her mother, Lucille Mabel Walthall Payne. Rice has published and received numerous awards for her original poetry.

Policy Staff Meeting . . .
Remembering the Nineties

For Anne, Barbara, and Janet

Pile high the snow, so this small dialogue
can be catalogued, and shelved. Around the Mall
the white flakes fall—swirling, rising, diving:
nature's winter air force of pelting ice
invades the secret tops of all government spots.

Today's glossy paradigms—alleged to be new—
were cleverly resurrected in "renaissance" think-offs
at Hilton Head weekends. Economy, jobs,
education,
health care: wonky old spuds on new Spodes
of power.
Policies are high-wire acts to win votes,
bridges of rhetoric stretched to the next century;
donors of note get overnight keys, quietly.
One by one, in Washington, champions of change
will scrub off a tarnished name and scout for allies,
when alibis won't stop descent in political
cement.

Beyond control of tables of talking brains,
snow graces the Capital in crystal rains.
Everywhere's seen nice Gnostic redeemer sparks
purifying public streets and parks.
They will silence all, as they steadfastly fall
upon this noisy, lame, tax-frisky game.

Robert A. Rickard

(b. 1937, Thomasville, N.C.), now retired from federal career service, writes poetry at home in Washington, D.C. and at Laetare, in the Northern Neck of Virginia, where living by the water and engaging the writing of others continue to nourish his spirit. He is a member of the Poetry Society of Virginia and his poetry has appeared in three previous volumes of *The Poet's Domain*.

Robert A. Rickard

Sailors' Log, September 16, 1972

Brisk wind across the sloop's port bow
pushed her north, from Solomon's Island,
as summer sun pulled light across
the sailors' eighth happy day at sea.
The anchor of the CAL 25—
like a guaranteed guest reservation—
was dropped at the head of Hudson Creek,
safe haven off Little Choptank River,
east of mighty Chesapeake Bay.

Brownie left the dingy first,
fast as a racehorse out of its gate,
splashing through water to shake onto land,
eager for her tardy constitutional.
She sniffed in the shade of giant oaks,
nosing her way to an old farm house—
Victorian, unpainted clapboard, abandoned.
Her sailing crew could not resist
her path, for closer exploration.

The empty house defied definition:
no furniture, or photographs;
no dishes, curtains, rugs, or clothes;
nothing to signal a form of life
before the thieves and vandals arrived.
Except upstairs at one room's closet,
where clues were strewn about the floor
as if intended for our discovery:
childhood games, drawings, mementos;
college textbooks, essays, journals;
news clips on military matters.
At length eyes startled at a name
upon a bronze grave marker, unused,
of a life granted in 1936

and taken back in 1965,
the house's sober Rosetta stone.

That night on the boat we rested, rocked
by gentle eddies under the stars,
sifting through time for this Hudson Creek son:
"Age 29 at the time of death . . .
seven years before reaching his shore . . . ."

Another decade passed before
his name was found, in Washington,
on the Viet Nam Memorial wall.

D. Jane Jumping

For My Niece

Pete, her hope, has angel wings.
See, each class, how light he springs
  across the mocking poles—
  hooves fluffing luffing sky,
  this thoroughbred a butterfly?

Mistress Jane has nerves of steel.
Watch her, wow, she's got this deal
  with fate, or gracious gods—
  head scrubbing sand-stoked air;
  heft saddle-waxing *derrière*?

Hey, my friends, divorce your bookies.
Why, pray tell, not chance these rookies
  who dare to thrill spent hearts—
  at summer shows, of course,
  is woman's place not on a horse?

Sacred Seconds

What matters most is not measurable,
Not the daily watch or dutiful repertoire.

Hourglasses overturned, sacred seconds cascade,
Echoes of eternity, unfinished dances,
Unclaimed chances humbled by choices and
remorse.

Craving significance, translucent selves
Await the never ending Present
That, in one moment, started all.

Dawn J. Riddle

Ms. Riddle was born in 1967, and raised with her identical twin in Portsmouth, Va. She earned her undergraduate and graduate degrees in sociology at Virginia colleges: Mary Washington and William & Mary, respectively. She now manages the Mansion on Main Bed & Breakfast in Smithfield; and enjoys hosting the Isle of Wight Writers' Group there.

Perennial in September

Was it a Monarch butterfly which lit
on the other side of the blossom,
or was it petals flickering in the wind
when the blossom flew away?

Tom Russell

(b.1935, Washington, D.C.) a retired administrative librarian, is a graduate of Kenyon College and of the University of Michigan. He studied with J.C. Ransom, John Ciardi, William Packard, and Ann Darr. His work appears in volumes 8, 11–14 and 16 of *The Poet's Domain*. Published in a number of other magazines and anthologies, he has given readings in seven states. A former officer of the Poetry Society of Virginia, he resides at Harrisonburg, Va.

Getting through Glass

Imagine there's a way
of getting through glass
without slivering you
or shattering the glass.

Imagine glass goes
all soft like gauze
to let you through.

See it turn into
a melting brume,
a silvery bright mist,
somewhat easy to get through,
cool and slickly sliding you.

And you legislating lightly,
not wishing to harm
the melting medium
accommodating you.

And if the new world
you pass into is
strange and will not yield,
take out another piece
of gleaming glass
and look through it,
grinning like the Cheshire Cat
as the world begins to turn
from backwards-higgledy-piggledy
into right-way-round again.

Mary Lynn Veach Sadler

a native North Carolinian, and former college president, has a B.A. from Duke and an M.A. and a Ph.D. from the University of Illinois. Her academic publications include five books and some sixty-eight articles, and she has edited thirteen books/proceedings and three national journals. Now a creative writer, she has won awards for short stories, novels, plays, creative non-fiction, and poems.

Who Would See Love Die

The bud that was born in the manger bed
was the rose that bloomed with a thorny head;
but the crown and the cross could in no way
thwart
the eternal dream of the lowly start.
And for every one who would see love die,
who would stand and chant his "Crucify!,"
there will always be the two or three
who would share the load to Calvary,
who grieve the gushings of innocent blood—
divine or human—in brotherhood;
and, humbly, through crowds who coldly condemn,
will come wise men to search for Bethlehem.

Shirley Nesbit Sellers

(b. 1926, Norfolk, Va.), retired teacher of the Norfolk public schools, resides in Norfolk, Va. where she is active in storytelling and story and poetry workshops. She has won numerous awards in The Poetry Society of Virginia and Irene Leach Memorial Contests. Ms.Sellers has published a chapbook, *Where the Gulls Nest: Norfolk Poems*, Ink Drop Press.

Learning

Climbing this mountain's sunny side,
The trail glows with shades of green.
Snow of trilliums everywhere,
Violets purple, yellow, white,
Crowding the path; and Bluets' "Quaker Ladies,"
Reminding one of Andrew Wyeth,
Star banks beside the running brook.
Oh everywhere is freshness, dazzle of birth.

This side of mountain, all is sun.
Triumphant now, the summit gained,
With sun rays pouring circumference round
We stand like gods in realms of light.
Away, away, on every side
The folded ridges horizon-stretch,
Their secret mysteries of green
Snaring souls with emerald lures, and ecstasy.

Downward we start, and with the sun,
Plunge ever deeper into shade.
The long descent draws always down,
The sense of sinking laps us round,
Sun and day draw to our close.
Our feet, our knees, breast high; we wade
Into twilight, into night.
Learning the mountain's darker side.

Peggy Shirley

(b. 1918, Manila, Philippine Islands) Due to home-schooling by mother while in Philippines, Peggy has had a life-long love of poetry. She has served as a public and an Army librarian. This is her first published poem. She lives in Williamsburg, Va. with her retired U.S. Army Lt. Colonel husband.

And God Said . . .

(with apologies to Ernesto Cardenal)

Wondrous is the Word!
It shatters silence.
It gives form to formlessness.
It radiates light out of darkness into
darkness.
It seeks response.
It exists in response.
It is response.
It defies response like waves of static.

The unuttered Word is silence—
silence and more than silence.
Silence is secret:
secrets kept secret divide
as surely as words uttered in anger.

Pythagoras measured the harmony of Word,
universal and rational.
Plato forged Word into dialogue,
kin of Hegel's dialectic,
among people themselves
formed by Word.

Poets, in imitation of primal utterance,
create palpable images
and infinite meanings
out of finite words.

Wondrous is the Word
and all its descendants,
parsed and conjugated.

Bruce Souders

(b.1920, Richland, Pa.) is a retired United Methodist minister and professor emeritus at Shenandoah University, Winchester, Va. He is author of two books of poems and numerous works in anthologies and journals; editor of a volume of poems by S. Gordon Link; writer of introductions to two collections of poems by Jane Hu; and resource leader for poets of all ages. His work has appeared in every issue of *The Poet's Domain* since volume 3.

To Live among Stones

She runs free,
flings to the stars one quick plea
that she might live among stones
when her bones settle sweetly

with the dust.
Running now, she cannot trust
this solid earth to hold her
or deter the flame that must

devour youth
consume her house, burn her roof.
What gods will hear her cries when
dappled, thin, she lives this truth?

There are none,
none to intervene, not one
to aid or mourn as the flames
lick and maim. Yet, like the sun

she will rise
silent, staring, ever wise
living mute among stones,
now her bones, without disguise.

Melissa Watkins Starr

(b.1959, Eden, N.C.) is a free lance writer and a graduate student at Old Dominion University.

Four People Sat in a Long-Ago Room

Four people sat in a long-ago room,
two men, a young woman, and I,
friendship's cool drinks in our smooth, moving
hands,
and a cold moon illumined the sky.

Four people stood in a long-ago room,
a young woman, two men, and I,
discussing our ages when the century would end,
as we bade our good evening goodbye.

Fifty years in the future! How far it seemed then!
(But time vanishes more quickly than light
passes away from a winter day's dusk
to be sealed in the dark depth of night)

Three people are remembered in a long-ago room,
a young woman and two stalwart men,
who grew old together as all live things do
in life cycles again and again.

Four people once toasted their friendship's
long stand.
The century is interred in time's tomb.
The ebony sky by a chill moon is lit
(and I'm the last one in the room).

Margaret Stavely

(b.1918, Easton, Md.) whose poem, "A Hope for Horses," featured in *The Chronicle of the Horse*, Middleburg, Virginia, March 7 issue, suggests the poem holds the record for the length of time between acceptance and publication–May 1997 to March 2003! In July, her poem *Patriot's Idyl* received Honorable Mention in the Daughters of the American Revolution's annual membership literary competition. Following emergency surgery on July fourth, Ms. Stavely is now home after a brief stay in a local rehabilitation and nursing home.

Margaret Stavely

Photograph

I found a photograph of me, a child,
seated in an old school desk, eyes sharp
behind round spectacles, arms folded, mouth
severe.
Small owl, hair scrappy and uncombed,
contemptuously she dares the camera lens.

The season is winter; she wears a tie
under her collar, ending in a bow,
and a warm sweater.

I know time's twisting program brings me back
to find her as time turns upon itself.
I am aware that in a malleable recess
of consciousness she knows at seven years
more than I know now
and spells out the special alphabet of life
in the sepia print within my hand,
intending the message for no one but me.

How strong my sudden feeling for this child;
how strange, delightful to be where she sits
forever in the Golden Eye of God!

To Richard

The Prince is never coming!
Only a mortal, ordinary man
Who helps do the dishes,
Cooks sometimes,
Mows the lawn,
Goes to work each day and brings
the money home,
Holds me when someone dies,
Goes on weekend adventures with me,
Tolerates my craziness and loves me in spite of it.
An ordinary man with a big heart,
a basically good soul—
And no damned white horse to feed
or clean up after!

Karen J. Traweek

followed her heart to Virginia in 1985 and has no plans to leave. She had work published in the 1970s; and in the 1980s she won first prize in a contest held by Day Spring card company, yet still did not return to writing. Now in her "empty nest years," Karen has reconnected with poetry as a form of therapy, to express her thoughts and feelings. She has had work published locally and on the West Coast.

Medea

When Medea wasn't idle, she was often homicidal,
She occupied herself with bloody thoughts.
When she was up to something it was usually
 a rum thing,
While she wasn't entertaining Argonauts.

One day as she was lurking in her laboratory,
 working
On a shipment of imported wool from Greece,
She spied a better cargo on a vessel called the Argo;
It was Jason looking for the Golden Fleece.

Now her father, he was ranting over being late
 in planting,
For he hadn't any flowers for his wreath,
So in spite of all entreaties, naughty, wicked
 King Aeetes
Bullied Jason into sowing dragon's teeth.

But Jason was no farmer, for the teeth turned
 into armor,
And the armor all at once was full of men,
And Jason, through his pallor said, "The better
 part of valor
Is to disappear and live to fight again."

So he took the golden mouton and he fled
 from all the shootin',
And he sailed away from Colchis with the tide,
But he found Medea with him, swaying gently
 to the rhythm,
As she cast her brother's body o'er the side.

Constance Tupper

(b. 1919, New York, N.Y.) is a visual artist who has lived in Charlottesville, Virginia for over 40 years. A member of The Poetry Society of Virginia, she has had poems published in volumes 2–19 of *The Poet's Domain* and in *Orphic Lute*. In 1976 she won a Merit Award from *Woman 's Day* magazine for her essay, "Women, Today and Tomorrow."Among her awards are an Honorable Mention in The Poetry Society of Virginia's 1999 annual contest, and in 2002, a second prize for three Haikus.

Constance Tupper

Now Medea, so they tell us, was exceptionally
jealous,
And fickle Jason had a roving glance.
When a captivating "nancy" seemed to catch
his passing fancy,
Medea, smiling sweetly, laid her plans.

She wove a little jacket and secreted in the
placket,
An ounce or two of distillate of lye.
And then, presenting this dress to her hus-
band's latest mistress,
She settled back to watch the lady fry.

Then she murdered Jason's scions and she fed
them to the lions,
And she shook the dust of Corinth from her
toes.
After that we find Medea's husband was
Aegeus.
He was Athens' King, as everybody knows.

Her skill was not forgotten. To Aegeus she
was rotten,
And on sorcery and demonry she throve.
Most scholars were astonished that she never
was admonished,
But was worshipped as a goddess in a grove.

Quiet Moments in the Womb of Rain

I lay quietly in bed
Secure in the warm womb of rain
Beating steadily on the roof
As if in the tropical jungle.
Heard somewhere in space
Was the moaning of the dove
And the cries of some unknown
Bird seeking refuge from the rain.

I finish my dream of storms
Rising floods and crumbling land,
Trying to keep above the rising waters.

The dry fields and hills
Reach out their tongues to drink every drop
And hoard the precious moisture
Like money in the vault
Of the aquifers—storehouses of nature.
The farmers thank the Lord
For responding to their prayers.
And the rains come on steady and quiet.
Then in the somewhere distance
The thunder rumbles
Like timpani drums rolling
In a heavenly orchestra.

The dogwood blossoms
Are silently shedding their flower crowns
Having bloomed forth in splendor.
Their flower drops lie on the ground
Among the rain drops
White relics of a glorious spring
And form a stark contrast
On the black wet Honda.
People huddle inside
Or under their umbrellas
Avoiding puddles in the street
And the wet lawn licks their boots.

Jack Underhill

has a B.A. from the University of California at Berkeley, M.A.s from Columbia University and Harvard's School of Government, and a Ph.D. from George Mason University; is retired after 42 years of Federal service; has written a number of books on new towns; for five years has been enrolled in the poetry workshop of George Mason's Learning in Retirement Institute; aspires also to wood sculpture and painting; is a practicing grandfather to six grandchildren; has three adult children and a wife of 42 short years.

Doña Maria

Doña Maria, hawk-nosed, black-eyed, no smiles,
came down from the mountain, from those
pine-filled,
heavy scented slopes, and billowing rush of
streams.
"The witch woman has come," the people cried.
"She will tell you if your green stalks will bear
corn
and if the new-born child will have good luck."
Read those white, bleached bones, Doña Maria.
"Compadres, give her tea and chili.
The witch-woman has come!"

Elizabeth Urquhart

(b.1924, Greeley, Co.) Studied English literature and history at the University of Iowa; later earned a master's degree at Old Dominion University, Va. For eighteen years, she was a reading specialist in the Hampton Va. city, schools. She writes poetry, and is interested in gardens, music, and wildlife. She is a member of the Williamsburg Poetry Guild and The Poetry Society of Virginia. Her poetry has appeared in four volumes of *The Poet's Domain*.

Elizabeth Urquhart

Circus Nuns

Sister Frances Marie, winsome smile,
close-cropped brown hair,
and Sister Agatha, well-rounded, with bright eyes
both in polyester skirts the color of strawberries,
and blue tennis shoes, have joined the circus;
traveling from Florida to Maine.
They want to work in a community;
the circus fills that need.
Find your way to their trailer,
past the shrunken head with the bared teeth,
past the fire-eating man.
In one of the bedrooms there is an altar,
with two hundred consecrated wafers.
the nuns celebrate the Eucharist
with all who wish to come.
Theirs is an all-loving forgiving God.
Sister Agatha cooks meals and takes tickets.
Sister Frances Marie's blunt fingers tie knots
in the thick ropes holding the tents up.
Now the circus people have a swear jar
which collects bad words at a quarter each.
The nuns have brought humor and love.
The fat lady embraces them,
the black striped tiger growls and purrs in his cage
the grey wrinkled elephant trumpets.
Sister Agatha says,
"Let the animals out of their cages,
we have love, we are free."

Edith R. White

(b.1923, Passaic, N.J.)
Storyteller, water color painter, book reviewer, Edith graduated from Vassar College and served two years in the Naval Reserve. Widow of Dr. Forrest P. White, pediatrician, she has four children, eight grandchildren, and is a librarian, and teacher. She lives in Norfolk, Va., and enjoys tennis, world travel, and poetry, of course.

Aran Isles Sweater

I gather the cardigan's coarse wool about me,
poke the wood buttons through hand-finished holes,
feel grateful for warmth of the rough-knitted
garment.
But a deep shiver chills me with sudden awareness
of sorrows and longings twined into the sweater.

Sheep farmers driven westward by enemy forces
fled to settle these bleak, barren islands of Aran.
The earth was a wasteland of cracked rock layers.
With chapped hands they fitted the stones into
dwellings,
piled up rock fences to enclose their pinched fields,
and battled cruel seas to provide a scant living.

While the men in small craft put out on the ocean,
women folk daily climbed down to the beaches
piled on their shoulders sacks of sand, kelp,
and seaweed,
and spread them on rock fields to dry and to
season.
They added their night soil and rinds of their
mealtimes,
dug in seeds of wild plants and sturdy salt grasses.
Slowly the rock fields began their greening,
watered by sea winds, nourished by sun.
At last one small lamb could be held in by
stone walls
to nibble and grow till its wool coat was shaggy.
Then came the springtime, time of sheep
shearing.
Coarse thread was spun, wound into long skeins.

Edith R. White

At twilight when pots and children were scrubbed
the good wife could sit out and knit in the
starlight,
eyes scanning the sea for her men folk in small
craft
returning at last with their net hauls of fish.

Each wife had a pattern knit into her jumper,
a unique set of stitches by which could be told
which family must claim a drowned fisher's body
washed up by the sea after a swift-striking storm.

I bought a warm sweater with good Irish punts
and found me a garment taut and evenly knit
that wrapped me in history, yearning, and sorrow,
the stories and dreamings of Ireland's true lilt.

yin

three red geraniums
from the garden

in clear water
a white Japanese bowl
on the kitchen counter

tended to by wife

Robert E. Young

(b. 1931, Philadelphia, Pa.) is a retired social worker and medical school professor. He lives in Virginia Beach, Va. His poems have appeared in *The Poet's Domain*, volume 17, *Virginia Adversaria, Powhatan Review, Chrysler Museum Ekphrasis, Visions, Nanduti, Pax India*, and *Voyager*. Other writings have appeared in *Portfolio, The Beacon, The Jung Society Newsletter*, and The Poetry Society of Virginia's *80th Anniversary Anthology*.

Foster Child

Is she the fly—sitting alone
In constant watch—ready to flee
At the first sign of contact?
Or is she the spider
Guarding her precious web of sanity
Devouring all in reach
To feed her fragile hopes?
Or is she just a little girl
Living in a fantasy world
Peopled by small children
At the beach or the circus
Images given to her by television
Of happy normal families?
Children she wants to have one day.
Or is she the caterpillar
Quietly consuming her fears
Waiting for the day
She may enter her fantasy cocoon
And emerge the butterfly
In confidence and beauty.
For sometimes dreams come true.

Evelyn Morgan Zemba

(b.1953, Johnstown, Pa.) makes her fifth appearance in *The Poet's Domain*. Her poems have been published in *Backroads*, University of Pittsburgh, Johnstown, Pa.; *The Bassettown Review; Sensations*; and *Lucidity*. She has won several awards from Laurel Arts Poetry Forum, Somerset, Pa. and served as judge for their Spring 1997 contest.

Evelyn Morgan Zemba

Escape à la Christie

On a particularly tiresome day
Fraught with exasperation,
I might dream of escape.
Perhaps to take a trip by train
On the Orient Express.
Transport myself back
To Gibson Girl days,
Serene and elegant,
Gloved and chapeaued.
I could surround myself
With the trappings of society:
Wine and tobacco
Leather and wood.
Drink in their scents as I
Daintily sip my tea,
My eyes reflecting
The antique gleam of brass.
Admired by men, but held aloof,
I would seem a fragile, china-faced doll.
Tip my head alluringly
And smile, genteel through exotic lashes.
Far away from daily troubles,
Waited upon, I could sit, queen-like,
While others smoothed my way,
At ease with the careless insouciance
Of regal superiority.

On such a day
Even murder could be dismissed
As a mere intrusion.

A Reminder

A butterfly in the cemetery
is a guest unannounced
wishing not to tarry.
But the quick sojourn
is a welcomed relief,
reminding those who walk
among the dead that
we too yet have wings.

Rabbi Israel Zoberman

(b.1945, Chu, Kazakhstan, USSR), ordained as a reform rabbi by the Hebrew Union College-Jewish Institute of Religion in 1974, has been rabbi to Congregation Beth Chaverim in Virginia Beach, Va., since 1985. His poetry and his translations from Hebrew have been published in CCAR *Journal*, *The Jewish Spectator*, *The American Rabbi*, *Moment*, and *The Poet's Domain*, volumes 5 through 20.

Eve

The slender teenager roams the
neighborhood not unlike a gazelle,
gazing at all things, living and inanimate,
with the wonder of innocence
that to some is a mere reflection of
her developmental condition.
To me she is Eve
in the Garden of Eden.

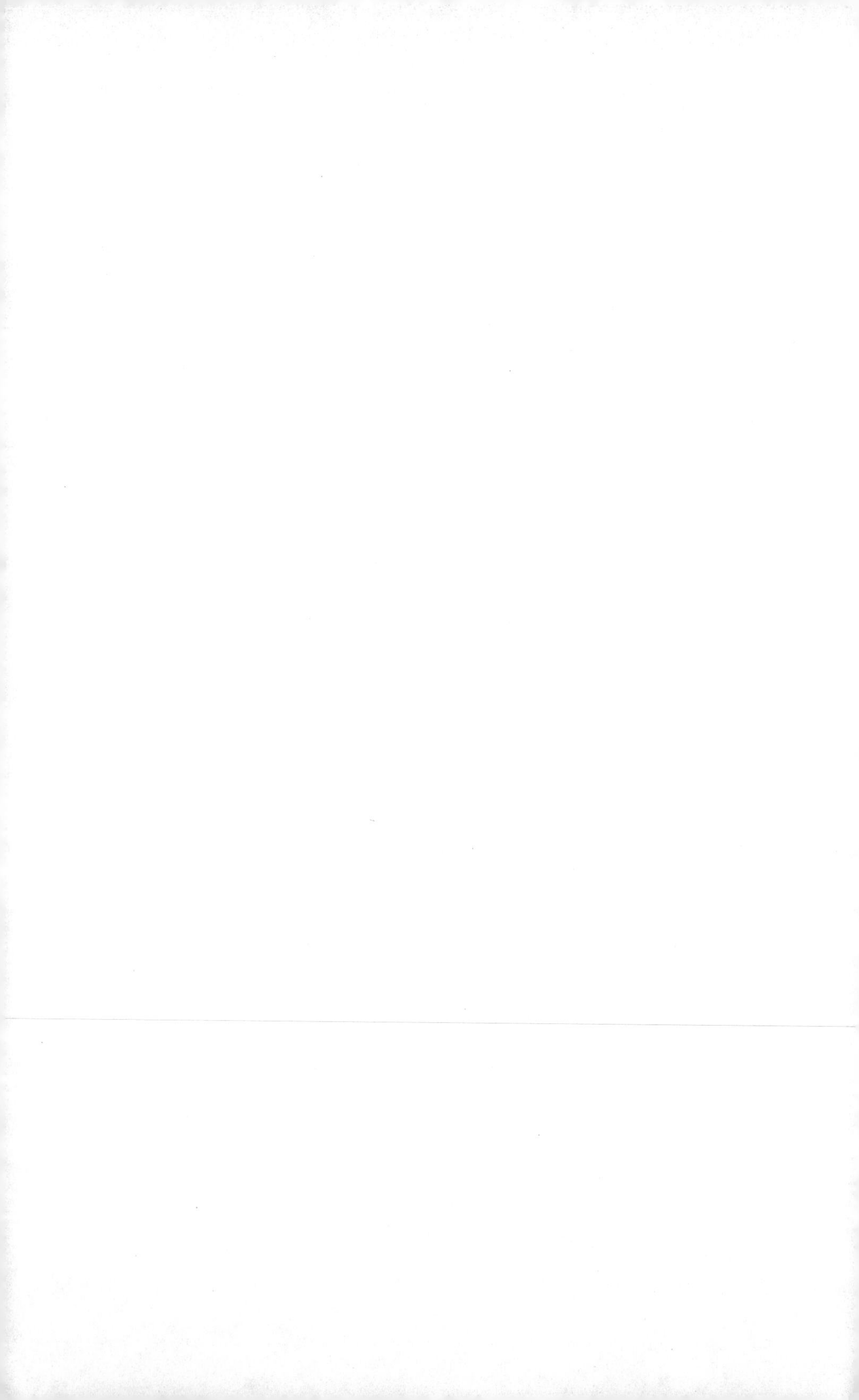